First World War
and Army of Occupation
War Diary
France, Belgium and Germany

58 DIVISION
Divisional Troops
Royal Army Veterinary Corps
58 Mobile Veterinary Section
25 January 1917 - 28 February 1919

WO95/2997/7

The Naval & Military Press Ltd
www.nmarchive.com
Published in association with The National Archives

Published by

The Naval & Military Press Ltd

Unit 10 Ridgewood Industrial Park,
Uckfield, East Sussex,
TN22 5QE England
Tel: +44 (0) 1825 749494

www.naval-military-press.com

www.nmarchive.com

This diary has been reprinted in facsimile from the original. Any imperfections are inevitably reproduced and the quality may fall short of modern type and cartographic standards.

© **Crown Copyright**
Images reproduced by permission of The National Archives, London, England, 2015.

Contents

Document type	Place/Title	Date From	Date To
Heading	WO95/2997/7		
Heading	58th Mobile Vety Section Jan 1917 Feb 1919		
Heading	War Diary Of 58 Mobile Vety. Sect		
War Diary	Sutton Remy	25/01/1917	25/01/1917
War Diary	Gn Route	26/01/1917	27/01/1917
War Diary	Frohen Le Gd	28/01/1917	05/02/1917
War Diary	Grouches Mill	06/02/1917	25/02/1917
War Diary	Humbercamp	26/02/1917	28/02/1917
War Diary	Mondicourt	29/03/1917	31/03/1917
War Diary	Grouches	01/04/1917	01/04/1917
War Diary	Frohen Le-Gd	02/04/1917	05/04/1917
War Diary	Amplier Bus-Les-As	06/04/1917	12/04/1917
War Diary	Bus-Les-Artois	13/04/1917	20/04/1917
War Diary	Bihucourt	21/04/1917	30/06/1917
War Diary	Roquigny	28/07/1917	31/07/1917
War Diary	Bihucourt	09/07/1917	09/07/1917
War Diary	Roquigny	10/07/1917	12/07/1917
War Diary	Bihucourt	02/07/1917	08/07/1917
War Diary	Rocquigny	01/08/1917	01/08/1917
War Diary	Fosseux	02/08/1917	27/08/1917
War Diary	In The Field	28/08/1917	31/08/1917
Heading	58 Division	07/10/1917	07/10/1917
War Diary	In The Field	01/09/1917	30/11/1917
War Diary	Field	01/12/1917	31/12/1917
War Diary	In The Field	01/02/1918	28/02/1918
War Diary	Field	01/03/1918	31/03/1918
War Diary	In The Field	01/04/1918	30/04/1918
War Diary	Neuville	01/05/1918	06/05/1918
War Diary	Hangest	07/05/1918	08/05/1918
War Diary	Pierregot	08/05/1918	17/05/1918
War Diary	Contay	18/05/1918	08/06/1918
War Diary	Reinneville	09/06/1918	10/06/1918
War Diary	Breilly	11/06/1918	18/06/1918
War Diary	Beaucourt	19/06/1918	04/08/1918
War Diary	Vignacourt	05/08/1918	08/08/1918
War Diary	Querrieu	09/08/1918	25/08/1918
War Diary	Heilly	26/08/1918	27/08/1918
War Diary	Morlancourt	28/08/1918	31/08/1918
War Diary	Bronfay Farm	01/09/1918	08/09/1918
War Diary	Bouchavesnes	08/09/1918	22/09/1918
War Diary	Map Ref D 14. B 8.1	22/09/1918	24/09/1918
War Diary	Map Ref D 14. B 8.1 62 B	25/09/1918	27/09/1918
War Diary	Mingoval	28/09/1918	30/09/1918
War Diary	Bouvigny	01/10/1918	15/10/1918
War Diary	Les Brebis	16/10/1918	18/10/1918
War Diary	Cite St. Pierre	19/10/1918	19/10/1918
War Diary	Montigny	20/10/1918	20/10/1918
War Diary	Moncheaux	21/10/1918	21/10/1918
War Diary	Bersee	22/10/1918	29/10/1918
War Diary	Nomain	30/10/1918	07/11/1918

War Diary	Rumegies	10/11/1918	11/11/1918
War Diary	Beloeil	13/11/1918	29/11/1918
War Diary	Peruwelz	30/11/1918	28/02/1919

WO 95/2997/7

58TH DIVISION

58TH MOBILE VETY SECTION
JAN 1917 – FEB 1919

WAR DIARY

OF

58 MOBILE VETY. SECT.

WAR DIARY or INTELLIGENCE SUMMARY

Army Form C. 2118.

58th Mobile Vety Section

Place	Date	Hour	Summary of Events and Information	Remarks and references to Appendices
Sutton Veny	25/6/1917		O/C 2 NCOs men & 2 ASC drivers left Sutton Veny for France on advanced party	
En Route	26/6/1917		with 24 horses	
"	27/6/1917		Arrived Southampton Camp Depot	
Rouen & Gd...	28/6/1917		Entrained for Rouen G. Station & proceeded to billets at Rouen Gd....	
"	29/6/1917			
"	30/6/1917			
"	1/7/1917		Received and treated sick & wounded of various units	
"	2/7/1917			
"	3/7/1917			
"	4/7/1917			
"	5/7/1917			
Gournay Road	6/7/1917		Section proceeded from Rouen Gd and to Gournay and Sortelem	1. Sec weekly returns in..... Rouen Reports etc not of interest
"	7/7/1917			do -
"	8/7/1917		Collection & treatment of animals of various units	do -
"	9/7/1917		for evacuation to Hospital &c	
"	10/7/1917			
"	11/7/1917			

W.R. Grivson Capt AVC
O.C. 58th M.V.S.

Army Form C. 2118.

WAR DIARY
or
INTELLIGENCE SUMMARY
(Erase heading not required.)

5th Mobile Vety Section

Place	Date	Hour	Summary of Events and Information	Remarks and references to Appendices
Corcelles	11/3/1917		⎫ Collection & treatment of animals of various units for Evacuation to Hospital &c. ⎬	
	12/3/1917			
	13/3/1917			
	14/3/1917			
	15/3/1917		Evacuation of Sick & Animals to Hospital in charge of NCO & 3 men from Bergueneuse – Abbeville	14 Bi-weekly Box Reports sent from 5th Section.
	16/3/1917			
	17/3/1917		⎫ Collection & treatment of Sick & Animals of Various units for Evacuation to Hospital &c. ⎬	17 {Bi-weekly Poor Reports sent Return of NCO & 3 men from Abbeville
	18/3/1917			
	19/3/1917			
	20/3/1917			
	21/3/1917			21 Bi-weekly Box Report sent
	22/3/1917		Evacuation of Sick & Animals to Hospital in charge of NCO & 3 men from Bergueneuse to Abbeville	
	23/3/1917			
	24/3/1917		⎫ Collection & treatment of Sick & Animals of various units for Evacuation to Hospital &c ⎬	24 {Bi-weekly Box Report sent Return of NCO & 3 men from Abbeville
	25/3/1917			

H. K. Ingrouille
Captain
M.V.S.
O.C. 5th

Army Form C. 2118.

WAR DIARY
or
INTELLIGENCE SUMMARY
(Erase heading not required.)

5th Mobile Veterinary Section
Vol 3

Place	Date	Hour	Summary of Events and Information	Remarks and references to Appendices
Humbercamps	26/2/1917		Section proceeded from GROUCHES to HUMBERCAMPS - Section links very sick and tired on arrival due to frost	
	27/2/1917		Collection & treatment of sick & horses from various Units	
	28/2/1917		do do Capt J.J. Robinson came to Section to take over Command from Capt W.E. Johnson AVC TF	
	1/3/1917		Evacuation of sick & animals from WARLINCOURT to ABBEVILLE 2d Reg Hospital 1.7.co and 3ra	
	2/3/1917		{ Watering of horses is a very difficult problem owing to total failure of the supply laid on by the Engineers. It was reported that the severe frost was the cause	
	3/3/1917		{	
	4/3/1917		Collection & treatment of animals from various units	
	5/3/1917		1 V.Co. O.R. ma proceeded to ABBEVILLE by road with 65 sick horses which to Belongea at advanced transport Depot for a horse float. Owing to the neglect movement of the spring & winter animals which was made of have been left their flight had been suffering + changes sustained. The attention of sick animals took a party number the sick two days & added responsibilities to various	
	6/3/1917			
	7/3/1917		Evacuation of 120 Sick & Animals from SAULTY-LARBRET to ABBEVILLE 17/co & 3rd mai. which includes 59 cases of debility and mange from Artillery Units attached to the Division.	
	8/3/1917			
	9/3/1917			
	10/3/1917		Collection and treatment of sick & animals from various Units	
	11/3/1917			
	12/3/1917		Evacuation of 66 sick & animals from SAULTY-LARBRET to ABBEVILLE 17.Co & 3rd mai	
	13/3/1917		Capt Johnson AVC TF proceeded to No 8 Veterinary Hospital	

J.J. Robinson CAPT. A.V.O.
O.C. 5th Mobile Vety. Sec.

WAR DIARY
or
INTELLIGENCE SUMMARY

Army Form C. 2118.

Place	Date	Hour	Summary of Events and Information	Remarks and references to Appendices
Ambleteuse	14/3/1917		Collection and treatment of Sick & Animals from various Units	
	15/3/1917			
	16/3/1917		Evacuation of 59 sick & animals from SAULTY-LARBRET & ABBEVILLE 1400am Train	
	17/3/1917			
	18/3/1917			
	19/3/1917		Collection and treatment of Sick & animals from various Units	
	20/3/1917			
	21/3/1917			
	22/3/1917		Evacuation of 111 Sick & animals from SAULTY-LARBRET & ABBEVILLE 1400am.	
	23/3/1917		Further batch of sick animals returned to unit taken by various Units	
	24/3/1917		Evacuation of 78 Sick & animals from SAULTY-LARBRET & ABBEVILLE 1400 - 9am This M.O. had detailed under instructions from ADVS from an Artillery Brigade	
	25/3/1917			
	26/3/1917		Collection of Sick & Animals from various Units. Evacuations are previously heavy. They are chiefly cases of debility which is probably due to great causes i.e. practically all horses are clipped. The division is only just come ahead and the weather has been extremely severe, no foot rations so received and now my rugs have not been replaced, one from all these affairs have been attached to the Section to help and the work which has had on the Division Evacuations are much 465 ems	

...CAPT. A.V.C.

WAR DIARY or INTELLIGENCE SUMMARY

Army Form C. 2118.

2/1st London Mob Vety Section
58th Division

Vol 4

Place	Date	Hour	Summary of Events and Information	Remarks and references to Appendices
HUMBERCAMP	26.3.17		Collection & treatment of sick animals	
	27 "		Evacuation of 63 horses & 4 mules from SAULTY - LAABRET to ABBEVILLE in charge of 1 N.C.O and 9 men (including men from the division of unit attached temporarily to the section).	
	28 "		The Section proceeded to MONDICOURT & billetted there. Billets had to be found (these were the standings) for horses were small, scattered. There had not been a section at MONDICOURT for nine	
MONDICOURT	29 "		months.	
	30 "		Collection of sick animals started immediately	
	31 "		Evacuation of 37 animals from MONDICOURT to ABBEVILLE in charge of 1 N.C.O & 3 men. Section left MONDICOURT and billetted for the night in GROUCHES, at which place and LUCHEUX several animals had been left by units, which had to be seen & dealt with, i.e. either collected, destroyed,	
GROUCHES	1.4.17		left in charge of sentries, or enquiries made. The Capt & Lieut M. de LONGEVILLE is wired for to proceed to the H.Q. of the 174th Infantry Brigade, which is on the move. He leaves early in the morning, 1 horse is loaned to him. The roads following the river through the valley are in a terrible condition.	
FROHEN-LE-G.	2.4.17		The section proceeded via DOULLENS to FROHEN-LE-GRAND.	
	3.4.17		About 40 remounts in charge of one of the divisional officers who had been to the BASE for them arrived at the section. Jnd officer moves on with 20 Wagg?? and issues them out to the units of the Division, as they are again proceeding in the direction of the "line". The rest are left with us & are distributed during the next 2 days	
	4.4.17		Evacuation of 12 horses & 2 mules from DOULLENS to ABBEVILLE in charge of 1 N.C.O & 1 man	
	5.4.17		Evacuation of 10 horses from DOULLENS to ABBEVILLE in charge of 1 N.C.O & 1 man. The evacuation party moves away before dawn as it is booked that DOULLENS before the section, which then proceeds to AMPLIER, where it is billetted for the night.	
AMPLIER	6.4.17		After the supply of water had failed, animals had to be taken to BERTRANCOURT, where water was obtained from a large pond. The watering of animals unable to walk through the mud was great difficulty. A water-cart would be a great	
BUS-LES-ART	7 "			
	8 "			
	9 "		adjunct to a mobile section.	
	10 "		Collection & treatment of sick animals	
	11 "			
	12 "			

H. Holworth
CAPT. A.V.C.
O.C. 58th LDN. DIV. MOBILE VETY. SEC.

WAR DIARY or INTELLIGENCE SUMMARY

Army Form C. 2118.

2/1st Lond. Mob. Vety Section
58th Division

Place	Date	Hour	Summary of Events and Information	Remarks and references to Appendices
BUS-LES-ARTOIS	13.4.17		Evacuation of 5 horses & 2 mules in charge 1 onr A.V.C. private & one attached man from ACHEUX to ABBEVILLE	
	14.4.17		Collection & treatment of animals which come from all units in the neighbourhood. The O.C. had Veterinary charge of animals of various units in the surrounding villages.	
	15.4.17			
	16.4.17		Evacuation of 7 horses & 1 mule in charge of 1 N.C.O. & 1 man despatched from ACHEUX to ABBEVILLE. A/Corporal Hooper had his Stripes taken from him for a minor offence.	
	17.4.17		Treatment & collection of cases. From some time until now the supply wagon had remained attached to the section. Two men Ptes Timberley & Robinson are appointed acting Lance-Corporals.	
	18.4.17		Evacuation of 8 horses & 3 mules in charge of 1 N.C.O. & one man from ACHEUX to ABBEVILLE	
	19.4.17		Collection & treatment of cases.	
	20.4.17		Evacuation of 2 horses & 6 mules (the 8 mules) horses were sent on from the 14th Reserve Park A.S.C. yesterday in charge of 1 N.C.O. & 1 man. The party were sent to ACHEUX station early in the morning and the Section moved away to BUS-LES-ARTOIS late in the morning & proceeded to BIHUCOURT where it billeted in a shift for the night. The whole of the personnel helping on carry shed.	
BIHUCOURT	21.4.17		The safety money into a position & the personnel are billeted in the carry forth for some time. Building is found in damaged state by hits by works of the red animal.	
	22.4.17		Collection & treatment of cases. 80 yards available for horses is pumped from the village pond.	
	23.4.17		is very poor indeed. It is earthy & smelly, & for this reason arrangements are made with "W" major of the W. forth to provide a daily supply of clean water by motor lorry forth. The Carps engineers provide three troughs for till the purpose, which are put into section Camp.	
	24.4.17		Evacuation of 40 horses & 6 mules from ACHIET-LE-GRAND to FORGES-LES-EAUX in charge of 1 N.C.O. and 4 men. Some large pistol cases are obtained from a battery of heavy gunners & use is kept in these, until the horses in billeting get it is hot thought advisable that method. The worst of them are Debility cases which suffered much on a long rail journey.	
	25.4.17		Collection & treatment of cases.	

H. Rushworth
O/C. 58th LDN. DIV. MOBILE VETY. SEC.

Army Form C. 2118.

WAR DIARY
INTELLIGENCE SUMMARY
(Erase heading not required.)

Instructions regarding War Diaries and Intelligence Summaries are contained in F. S. Regs., Part II. and the Staff Manual respectively. Title Pages will be prepared in manuscript.

21 London Mobile Vety Section - 58th Divn.

Sheet I   Vol 5

Place	Date	Hour	Summary of Events and Information	Remarks and references to Appendices
BIHUCOURT	26.4.17		Collection & treatment of cases. As many animals as possible are kept in the Section until they are recovered when they are returned to their unit. There is a great shortage of remount so that every effort is made to return animals to their units.	
	27.4.17		Evacuation of 37 horses & 4 mules from ACHIET-LE GRAND to FORGES-LES-EAUX, 38 belonging to this division. Water is still to be sent in large bottles with the animals in the trucks, although watering arrangements are now made at one or two halts down the line. Reports are brought back that they shunting by the french railway authorities is done much more carefully, with the result that it is very seldom now that an animal goes down & cast that cannot be got up. This time O/C Pte Hayles the Clerk to the Section is learnt to the A.D.V.S as his clerk has been removed to hospital.	
	28.4.17			
	29.4.17		The usual routine	
	30.4.17		Evacuation of 15 horses from ACHIET-LE GRAND to FORGES-LES-EAUX. No 7 Veterinary Hospital all belonging to this division. North Hides are sent with them parties as they all proved evacuation are by much lighter. There is very little infectious disease about, the worst cases are the result of chilled extremities & necrotic dermatitis which responds fairly readily to treatment. After some time a number of cases of Ulcerative Cellulitis, though there do not appear to be treatment & in one unit two cases of gangrene and necrosis set in in the extremity. Debility cases received about the end of April & early days of may were also suffering from exhaustive & severe becomes of dermatitis.	
	1.5.17			
	2.5.17			
	3.5.17		The usual routine	
	4.5.17		A slight mishap happens to the horse float - one of the spring brackets breaks, which is not difficult to get repaired, the piece cannot be replaced as it is a french made vehicle. The O.C. 62nd (WR) M.V.S. is good enough to lend me his float on several occasions. 14 horses & 2 mules were evacuated today, 1 animals belonging to this division.	
	5.5.17			
	6.5.17			
	7.5.17			
	8.5.17		The usual routine & also the painting of the vehicles of the Section.	

WAR DIARY
INTELLIGENCE SUMMARY

Army Form C. 2118.

2/1 London Mobile Vety.
Section – 58th Division

Sheet II

Place	Date	Hour	Summary of Events and Information	Remarks and references to Appendices
	5.5.17 6.5.17 7.5.17 8.5.17 9.5.17		About these dates the winter clothing was being handed in to the O.C of the division.	
	10.5.17		Inoculation of a batch of NCOs & men with first injection of T.A.B takes place this day. They are excused duty for 30 hours. The establishment of Riding Horses of the Section is temporarily reduced, 5 horses are handed to the Divisional Artillery, in accordance with instructions from Remount Dept. through D.H.Q. The 5 sets of saddlery were handed over to the Ordnance Officer.	
	11.5.17		A Riding Mare sent into the Section gives birth to a filly-foal. 19 horses were evacuated to Base Hospital this day. 2nd batch of NCOs & men were inoculated with 1st dose of T.A.B & excused duty for 30 hours.	
	14.5.17 15.5.17 16.5.17		Last batch of NCOs & men were inoculated this day as above. Collection & treatment of animals. The excellent weather experienced lately has made it possible to give the cattle good grazing. A Boyes Stove is issued to the Section for cooking food for the sick cattle.	
	17.5.17 18.5.17		The O.C. Capt. J. Richmond commences his leave to England this day & departs at 8. 0 a.m. Capt. J. Scott-Bowden – A.V.C. takes over command of the Section on this date. Evacuation of 21 horses & 1 mule evacuated to Hospital this day – 16 animals belonging to 58" division.	
	19.5.17		Inoculation of a batch of NCOs & men with 2nd dose of T.A.T.B there being no ill effects consequent.	
	20.5.17 21.5.17 22.5.17		2nd Batch of NCOs & men inoculated as above Collection & treatment of cattle. Evacuation of 14 horses to Veterinary Hospital – 9 belonging to 58th Division. Last batch of NCOs & men inoculated today with satisfactory results.	
	23.5.17 24.5.17 25.5.17		Collection & treatment of cases. 4 horses of 58th Division evacuated to Hospital today.	

J.Scott-Bowden, Capt
O.C. 58. M.V.S

WAR DIARY
or
INTELLIGENCE SUMMARY

Army Form C. 2118.

(7)

Place	Date	Hour	Summary of Events and Information	Remarks and references to Appendices
BIHUCOURT	29.5.17		Capt. & J. RICHMOND. D.P.C. returned from leave. 15 horses (one mare with foal at foot) + 1 mule evacuated from ACHIET LE GRAND to N°7 Veterinary Hospital FORGES LES EAUX.	SB
	30.5.17		2 men received 2nd inoculation. This completes T.A.B. inoculation of all personnel of the Section. Capt. & J. RICHMOND, A.V.C. posted to 291st Brigade R.F.A. Capt. J. SCOTT BOWDEN, A.V.C (T.F.) posted to command the Section.	SB

J S Bowden Capt
Capt "D" in M.V.S.
SS

WAR DIARY or INTELLIGENCE SUMMARY

Army Form C. 2118.

2/1 (London) Mobile Vety. Section — Page 10 — Vol 6

Place	Date	Hour	Summary of Events and Information	Remarks and references to Appendices
BIHUCOURT	1/6/17		One of the 14 horses a R Bay mare + a stray animal, Evacuated to 7 Vety Hospital FORGES LES EAUX on 22-5-17 for Cellulitis of back. Proved to be Glandered, all possible in contacts totalling 41, were Segregated to be tested with Mallein in 21 days.	SCV3
"	2/6/17		12 Horses + 4 Mules were today evacuated to 7 Vety Hospital. 11 of them belonged to 58" Division. Several large calibre high explosive shells dropped on both sides of the Section lines, all animals here got away there were no casualties.	SCV3
"	3/6/17		Return of Shipping saved for Month of May amounted to 70 lbs of "A" Quality.	SCV3
"	5/6/17		17 Horses + 1 Mule evacuated to 7 Vety Hospital, 11 of them from This Division.	SCV3
"	7/6/17		Section moves to new camp in same village map reference Sheet 57C. B.17.B.5.7 a very suitable site.	SCV3
"	8/6/17		5 Horses 24 Mules evacuated to 7 Vety Hospital, 8 from This Division.	SCV3
"	10/6/17		Dr Farrier returned from a fortnight's leave at V Corps Summer rest camp at ST VALERY-SUR-SOMME.	SCV3
"	12/6/17		S/Sergt Alden. W. granted 15 days long Service leave, the second 15 days due to him to be taken later. 14 horses evacuated to 7 Vety Hospital. 7 from This Division. 6 of these came new mange suspects, one belonging to This Division. 21 Glanders in contact animals tested with Mallein at expiration of 21 days	SCV3

Lieut M Rowden TF
Capt A.V.C TF
O.C. "8" Div M.V.S.

WAR DIARY or INTELLIGENCE SUMMARY

Army Form C. 2118.

2/1 (London) Mobile Vety. Section. Page 11.

Place	Date	Hour	Summary of Events and Information	Remarks and references to Appendices
BIHUCOURT	13.6.17		Of the 21 animals tested with mallein yesterday all gave negative reactions. 19 Section Horses & 1 inoculated charger tested with mallein at expiration of 21 days after possible incontact with evacuated Glanders case.	SD/3
"	14.6.17		17 animals that had been undertreatment in the Section were returned to their respective units. The 20 animals tested yesterday with mallein gave negative reactions. Gas Alert signal at 12.30 a.m. 8 horses & 2 mules evacuated to No.7 Vety Hospital FORGES-LES-EAUX. 9 from this Division	SD/3
"	15.6.17		ACHIET LE GRAND Station shelled by enemy high Explosive Shells during the entraining. No casualties to Section men or horses.	SD/3
"	19.6.17		13 horses evacuated to No.7 Vety Hospital, 5 from this Division. 1 Mule sent to Base.	SD/3
"	21.6.17		7/4/233767. Dr. Dickinson T. A.S.C. 1st Line driver attached to the Section granted one month's furlough on account of long service. He has been temporarily replaced by T/4/237766. Dr. Nicks J.E.M. from 509 Coy A.S.C.	SD/3
"	22.6.17		5 horses & 2 mules evacuated to No.7 Vety Hosp.	SD/3
"	23.6.17		T/T0846 a/cpl MAYLAR A.V.C. granted 10 days special leave on account of severe illness of his father.	SD/3
"	26.6.17		22 Horses 2 mules evacuated to No.7 Vety Hosp, 12 of them from this Division including 1 Remount case a mule being returned for further training. J.W.A. Bowden F. Cr./F. A.V.C. O.C. 56th Div M.V.S.	SD/3

WAR DIARY 2/1 (London) Mobile
or Vety. Section 12
INTELLIGENCE SUMMARY

Army Form C. 2118.

(Erase heading not required.)

Place	Date	Hour	Summary of Events and Information	Remarks and references to Appendices
BIHUCOURT	29.6.17		14 horses & 1 mule evacuated to No 7 Vety Hospital, 9 of them belonging to this Division	
"	30.6.17		A/S/Sergt Alden M. returned to duty on expiration of leave.	

J.A. Bowden Cpt. A.V.C.
O.C. 2/1 Lond.
Div. M.V.S.

Army Form C. 2118.

88 Div Wks
Sheet No 17

WAR DIARY
or
INTELLIGENCE SUMMARY
(Erase heading not required.)

Instructions regarding War Diaries and Intelligence Summaries are contained in F. S. Regs., Part II. and the Staff Manual respectively. Title Pages will be prepared in manuscript.

Place	Date	Hour	Summary of Events and Information	Remarks and references to Appendices
Royencourt	28.7.17		2 Stray Horses brought into these lines by Headquarters IV Corps at 5.30 p.m. duly notified for immediate Sec Fontaine Gerard.	
"	29.7.17		A.F. B.213. rendered to Headquarters 58 Division.	
"	30.7.19		Inf/23.776 Lr Fuchs J.S.M. A.S.C. returns to Coy Hqs. #7 a.S.B. for duty.	
"	31.7.17		Pioneer Purdy leave for 7st furlough daily ration at Lozinne.	

Royencourt
31.7.17.

C.H. Sheather Capt. A.V.C.
Oc 58 Div M.T. Section.

WAR DIARY or INTELLIGENCE SUMMARY

Army Form C. 2118.

3rd Div M.V.S.

Sheet No. 16.

Place	Date	Hour	Summary of Events and Information	Remarks and references to Appendices
Rouxmesnil	24.7.17		5 Horses & 2 Mules dispatched to Forges-les-Eaux, in charge of one N.C.O. & 2 animals belonging to the 65 Bn. V.G.	
"	25.7.17.		S/S 9388 Pte. Sargeant W. G. reports sick at this station for duty. This man returns off Pass Hospital from No 2 Vety Hospital, Havre. R.A.V.C. who was admitted to hospital in England etc. for him. Letter received through D.A.D.V.S. re shortage of mules received on journey for 58 Horses evacuated to Forges-E-Eaux. Letter sent to off. i/c D.A.V.D. explaining the original receipt which should read – "16 and not 2 as stated on receipt."	
"	26.7.17		Weekly Returns rendered to D.A.D.V.S. & forwarded to A.D.V.S. Strength Last Return 53. admitted since 27 total 80. Evacuated 50. Died 10. Remaining 20. Total 80. Evacuation of 26 Horses & 5 Mules from Rouxmesnil to Forges-les-Eaux. 23 animals from 58 Bn. Vety. accompanies horses in 10. cattle trucks.	
"	28.7.17		Patrol Paris.	

Rouxmesnil
31. 7. 19 19.

Capt. Shaxer
Sept 8.H.C.
O.C. 3. Div M.V.S.

Army Form C. 2118.

WAR DIARY or **INTELLIGENCE SUMMARY**

58 Div M.V.S — Shut N° 15

(Erase heading not required.)

Instructions regarding War Diaries and Intelligence Summaries are contained in F.S. Regs., Part II and the Staff Manual respectively. Title Pages will be prepared in manuscript.

Place	Date	Hour	Summary of Events and Information	Remarks and references to Appendices
Roguigny	14.7.17		17 Horses & 3 Mules evacuated from Roguigny to Forges-les-Eaux. 16 animals belonging to 58 Division. Khaki is again carried in & Sabtin Bobot this, as a supply of empty cartridge cylinders is not available.	
"	15.7.17 / 16.7.17		Collection & treatment of cases.	
"	17.7.17		21 Horses & 2 Mules evacuated to Forges les Eaux from Roguigny. 24 animals from 58th Division.	
"	18.7.17		Usual Routine.	
"	19.7.17		H.E. 1863. Happgt Cotton. F. a V.C. arrives for duty from H. 1. H. V.S. thus completing our Establishment of two Vety Section.	
"	20.7.17		1.7.07.12 Pho. Sgt. Dausé. E. a V.C. granted 10 days Special Leave on account of serious family illness.	
"	21.7.17		Evacuation of 113 horses from Roguigny to Forges-les-Eaux. 7 animals belong to the 58 Division.	
"	22.7.17		Usual Routine. 770809 Pte Bourn. C.E. a.V.S. Reports to Section on his return from III Army General Rest. Camp.	
"	24.7.17		H. Dobinson. J. a V.S. is sent to join his unit, Roguigny 58 D.V.S, but with a letter from C.O. asking for his stay w us with a view that instruction for Horseshoers m.y. be given. If that cannot be arranged. Ch. letter referred for J.C.P.V.S.	

C.H. Sheatnew
Capt 58 Div M.V.S.

Roguigny 31.7.17.

Army Form C. 2118.

WAR DIARY
or
INTELLIGENCE SUMMARY

38" Div M.V.S.   Sheet No. 14.

(Erase heading not required.)

Instructions regarding War Diaries and Intelligence Summaries are contained in F. S. Regs., Part II. and the Staff Manual respectively. Title Pages will be prepared in manuscript.

Place	Date	Hour	Summary of Events and Information	Remarks and references to Appendices
Béhencourt	9.7.17		The Section proceeds via Bohavesne & to Travesloy to Rogrigny, leaving Béhencourt at 8.50 am arriving at new camp at 3 p.m. (Map Ref Sheet 57 b. 037. d 99.) Section halted en route, beyond Béhencourt for watering & feeding of animals. 3 Tents & G.S. taken over from 19 L Mod Vety Section at Rogrigny. This Section affords excellent opportunities for watering horses alongside water point & troughs.	
Rogrigny	10.7.17		Erection of suitable lines, road making & treatment of cases.	
"	11.7.17		Farriage Return rendered 6-T a 5 V.S. Collection & treatment of cases. Imprest account & balance J. cash handed over to Capt. Sheather by Major Scott Bowden J. S. a. & V.S. Balance as per A.P.M.1513 a. = £47 7s. 03/4. Payments &c. Glauberr Horse Powse notified. A special Section's Farriage Return rendered to D.A.D.V.S.	
"	12.7.17		General venture. AF. 0.689. Pte Thompson H.A.D.G.J. M.V.S. evacuated to III Corps Rest Station with knee trouble. Weekly Returns submitted to D.A.D.V.S. & approved.	

Rogrigny
12.7.1917

C. H. Sheather
Capt. A.V.C.
O.C. 38 Div. M.V.S. with dutch feeling.

WAR DIARY
or
INTELLIGENCE SUMMARY

Army Form C. 2118.

58th Div Mob Vety Sect

Sheet N° 13

Place	Date	Hour	Summary of Events and Information	Remarks and references to Appendices
BIHUCOURT	2.7.17		Selected cases for Evacuation to Base Hospital.	2013
	3.7.17		26 Sick Animals Evacuated from ACHIET LE GRAND to N° 7 Vety. Hospital FORGES-LES-EAUX 16 of these belonged to 58th Div. Males for journey carried in Empty Cartridge Cylinders.	2013
	5.7.17		Weekly returns forwarded to D.A.D.V.S. Showing Last Return 70. Total 109. Cured 3. Transferred Sick 43. Died nil. Destroyed nil. Remaining 63. Total 109.	2013
	6.7.17		Evacuation of 23 animals from ACHIET LE GRAND to N°7 Vety Hospital FORGES LES EAUX. 16 of these belonged to 58th Div. Local orders A.V.C. N° 66 received dated 3.7.17. received showing T.T.0801. P/A/Sgt. ALDEN, M. appointed A/cn.W. of P/A/Staff/Sgt with effect from 3.7.17. according to M.V.S. new War Establishments.	2013
	7.7.17		Notification by O/C A.V.C. Records Woolwich, sen. O/c A.V.C. Base Records that T.T.0546 L/A/Cpl HAVILLAR who whilst on 10 days Special Leave to England 23.6.17 – 3.7.17 had been admitted Mil. Imar Hospital CROYDON suffering from Tonsilis of ago.	
	8.7.17		Capt C.H. SHEATHER A.V.C. returned for duty on appointment as O.C. 58 Div M.V.S. Accordingly handed over Command & term of balance in hand/duplicate/ advance pay with A.S.C. Supply wagon leave for 42nd Div M.V.S a/c Recovery.	2013

BIHUCOURT
8.7.17.

Neil W Bowden
Major A.V.C.
O.C. 58 Div M.V.S.

WAR DIARY
INTELLIGENCE SUMMARY

Army Form C. 2118.

Wks I Wk Vely See
J of 8

Place	Date	Hour	Summary of Events and Information	Remarks and references to Appendices
Rocquigny	Aug 1st	8.30 am	The Section proceeds, via Le Transloy, BEAULENCOURT, BAPAUME, ACHIET-LE-GRAND to ABLAINZEVELLE arriving at 3.30pm. Section halted for night, Tempy lines are made & the men bivouac in an open field.	
FOSSEUX	Aug 2nd		The Section proceeds at 9am through AYETTE, ADINFER, RANSART, BELLACOURT, BEAUMETZ-LES-LOGES, MONCHIET, GOUY-EN-ARTOIS, arriving at FOSSEUX at 3pm. Map ref. 51c. P.C.8.5. Took over standings previously occupied by 6 M/m M.V.S. Condition of standings passable. Surrounding ground waterlogged & unsanitary, accommodation for 40 animals. — T.T. 0656. Pte. J. RACKHAM proceeds on 10 days special leave to U.K.	
	3rd		Ordinary routine. Weekly returns rendered to DDVS, approved 1 NCO & 2 men return from base from conducting evacuated animals.	
	4th		A.F. B.213 rendered to H.Q.	
	5th		T.T. 0713. Pte. HEASMAN.D.G. proceeds to St Valery Rest camp in acc with III Army Memo. A5/5051. for 15 days.	
	6th		T.T. 0689. Pte. THOMPSON.K.H. reported from 41st Sty Hospital & is taken on the strength. Return of Antigas appliances to DADOS. — advance of each to all NCO's & men.	
	7th		T.T. 0712. P/q/Sgt. E. DOUST. AVC. returned off 10 days special leave to U.K. This NCO returned via HAVRE and was 6 days delayed there awaiting train transport.	

WAR DIARY
or
INTELLIGENCE SUMMARY

Army Form C. 2118.

Place	Date	Hour	Summary of Events and Information	Remarks and references to Appendices
FOSSEUX	Aug. 7		Evacuation to No 22 Vet Hospital ABBEVILLE, from GOUY-EN-ARTOIS, 1 horse, 2 mules, 1 NCO 1 man i/c.	
	8		S.E. 23850. Pte H. ABRAHAMS A.V.C. reported from No 1. VET. HOSPITAL and to taken on the strength, this man was to replace T.T. 0689 Pte H THOMPSON, A.V.C. who was evacuated sick out of the Divisional Area but returned here for duty, before the reinforcement arrived. Section now 1 Pte surplus.	
	8		Inspection of Section by Lt. COL. B.L. LAKE A.D.V.S.	
	9		One BK Jack Mule recovered from in RAMBAUX FARMER. WAGONLIEU appearently abandoned, condition poor and suffered mange. Weekly returns rendered to D.A.D.V.S. & approved.	
	10		Medical inspection of knowlegen personnel of the unit for class y ration A.F. B.213. & weekly strength return rendered to D.A.D.V.S.	
	11		EVACUATION to 22. Vet HOSPITAL. 2 Horses 2 mules 1 NCO in charge. Issue of clothing to all men and NCO's of Section. 1 BK Bay Jenny Mule found & brought into the section by Air 1/2 B. C Field Ambulance, D.A.D.V.S. A.P.M. duly notified.	
	12		1 NCO + 2 Men were dispatched for duty with XVII Corps Horse Rest Camp via ace with XVII Corps memo A 54/4.b.	

WAR DIARY
of
INTELLIGENCE SUMMARY
(Erase heading not required.)

Army Form C. 2118.

Vol. VII

Place	Date	Hour	Summary of Events and Information	Remarks and references to Appendices
FOSSEUX.	Aug 13	T.T. 0716	Pte W. FORD. A.V.C. despatched to XVII Corps horse rest camp to relieve T.T. 0809. Pte C.C. DAWES. A.V.C. who has been ordered to return to his section	
	14	T.T. 0809	Pte C.C. DAWES. A.V.C. is despatched to No 2 Vet Hospital, in acc with O/c Records circular memo 7/129/16. Surplus to establishment. No 1762.2. Gr J NISBET No 1 Sec DAC. 58" DIV. + No 218461. D/C. GREENWOOD. D/B41 291 Bde RFA. more this day returned to their respective units.	
	16.		Westley returns indoors to D.A.D.V.S. + approved. Bkmare 15.2 aged. found + brought into section by camp commandant XVII Corps. D.A.D.V.S. + A.P.M. notified. (Suspected mange case)	
	17.	No 63791	Dr BANCROFT. G. M.G.C passed out capable of performing duties of cold shoer + returned to 214 MGC for duty.	
	18.		Bay mare. 15-3. aged. found + brought to section by 7/9 London Regt D.A.D.V.S. and A.P.M. notified. Evacuation to No 22 Vet Hospital, (animals in charge 1 NCO. AF. B 2135 mange cartage returns rendered to D.A.D.V.S. approved)	
	20.	No T.T. 0731	Pte HEASMAN. D.G. returns from St Valery Rest Camp for duty.	

WAR DIARY or **INTELLIGENCE SUMMARY**
(Erase heading not required.)

Army Form C. 2118.

Shul. IV

Place	Date	Hour	Summary of Events and Information	Remarks and references to Appendices
FOSSEUX.	AUG 21		Routine.	
	22		Evacuated 10 horses & 2 mules to ABBEVILLE from GOUY-EN-ARTOIS. 1N.C.O + 1 Man in charge.	
	23		Weekly Returns rendered to D.A.D.V.S. and approved.	
	23.		T.T. 0731 Pte HEASMAN. D.S. and TT0656 Pte RACKHAM. J. have medical exam with a view to transfer to combatant units.	
	24		T.T. 0874 A/Cpl. CURBISHLY. P. TT0716 Pte FORD H. TT0757 Pte HOOK J. return this day from duty with the XVII Corps Horse Rest Camp.	
	25.		The Section leaves FOSSEUX at 4.30 a.m. & proceeds by HAUTEVILLE, HERMAVILLE to AUBIGNY, arriving at latter place 6.45 am & entrains at 7am. Arrives at HOPOUTRE 5.30 pm proceeding by road to Camp. F22. C.4.6. Sheet 27 N.E.	
	26		No 390163 Pte MARTIN. H.A 2/9 LONDON. Regt. is returned to DIV N H Q for duty.	
	27.		21675 Pte. DAY.H. A.S.C. att 2/2 H.C. Field Amb. & No 3217 44 Pte PINCHING.F. 2/6 LONDON Regt. are returned to their units for duty. Bay mare collected & conveyed in float from 2/1st H.C. Field Amb. to M.V.S.	

WAR DIARY or INTELLIGENCE SUMMARY

Army Form C. 2118.

Sheet V

Place	Date	Hour	Summary of Events and Information	Remarks and references to Appendices
In the field	28/8/17		T.T.0646. Pte FURBER. F. A.V.C. Admitted 2/3 H.C. Field Amb. N.Y.D.	
	29/8/17		The Section left camp at F.22. C.46. Sheet 27. N.E. at 9am. & proceeds by A.28. D.98. map 28 arriving at 12.30pm. Horse wounded & reported to Corps mobile at Proven.	
	30"		SE.1863 Ph/Sgt Cotton F. AVC. proceeds to 174 Inf. Bde. for duty vice Sgt MAYNARD on leave.	
	31st		Evacuation of 17 horses to Corps Mobile Vet Section, MOLEN PROVEN Inspected by DADVS prior to moving. Weekly returns rendered & approved.	
	31st		T.T.0871 S/Smith Stewart J. A.V.C. admitted to 1/3 (H) Field Amb. N.Y.D. 1 Hide sent to Corps Mobile.	

G/d Sheathin Capt
O.C. 58th Divl. M.V.S

A.Q.
"A"
58 Division

[Stamp: 58th (LONDON) DIVISION (VETERINARY) Date V/2/115]

Herewith War Diary of 58 Div. M.V.S. for the month ending Sept 30/17. It is regretted that this was not at H.Q. by the 1st inst but owing to an error same had to be returned and was delayed through the post.

M. J. Glyn
Capt A.V.C.
Major,
g. A.D.V.S.
58th (LONDON) DIVISION.

A+Q
7-10-17.

WAR DIARY
or
INTELLIGENCE SUMMARY

Army Form C. 2118

D.A.D.V.S. & Supt Vety Sec
58th Division
9/1 L.M.V.S.
9 of 9

Place	Date	Hour	Summary of Events and Information	Remarks and references to Appendices
In the Field	Sept 1.17		Routine. T.T.0647 Pte FURBER. F. A.V.C. returned to duty from hospital	
	2.9.17		2/3rd Field Amb. Evacuation to Corps Mobile Vet Section 47 animals, 1 Mule – No 926268 Dr RUSHWORTH. E. – D Bac. 290 Bde R.F.A. returned to unit 1/c Bay. Good for Duty.	
	3.9.17		Routine	
	4.9.17		Routine	
	5.9.17		T.T.0871 Ssm STEWART. J. A.V.C. returned to duty from Corps Rest Station. Each advance to all NCOs & Men of Section Evacuation of 5 animals to Corps Mobile Vet Section SE 18631 P/A/Sgt COTTON. F. A.V.C. evacuated to BASE	
	6.9.17		Collection & treatment of cases carried through by float. Evacuation of 20 animals to Corps Mobile Vet Section.	
	7.9.17		Weekly returns to 8.A.D.V.S. submitted & approved.	
	8.9.17		Evacuation of 43 animals to C.M.V.S. at PROVEN. 1 Float case	
	9.9.17		Evacuation of 17 animals to C.M.V.S. at PROVEN. 4 Ambulances	
	10.9.17		No 60936 Dr MIDDLETON. P. passed as COLD SHOER and returned to 206 M.G.C.	
	10.9.17		Evacuation 12 horses 1 Mule to C.M.V.S at PROVEN.	
	11.9.17		1 P/o/opt and 11 men bathed & clothing changed 2 float cases admitted	
	12.9.17		SE 9368 Pte SERGEANT. M. 07 M.V.S commences 10days leave "Havre"	
	13.9.17		Evacuation of 34 animals to C.M.V.S. ceases by Ambulance, 3 horses " 3 " "	
	14.9.17		T.T.0639 commences 12days leave to Winny Rest camp.	
	15.9.17		Weekly returns rendered to 8.A.D.V.S. and approved. Payment of NCOs and men	

C.H. Shenton Capt AVC

Army Form C. 2118.

WAR DIARY
or
INTELLIGENCE SUMMARY
(Erase heading not required.)

2/1st LONDON M.V.S.   58th DIVISION.

Instructions regarding War Diaries and Intelligence Summaries are contained in F. S. Regs., Part II. and the Staff Manual respectively. Title Pages will be prepared in manuscript.

Place	Date	Hour	Summary of Events and Information	Remarks and references to Appendices
In the Field	15.9.17		3 Float cases admitted. A.F. B213 FIELD RETURN. rendered & approved	
	16.9.17		Evacuation of 55 Animals to C.M.V.S. BOWEN. 2 by MOTOR Ambulance	
			1 by FLOAT. — 1046 P/A/Sgt. ELLISON reports from DUTY at M.V.S. from N°6 Vet HOSPITAL.	
	17.9.17		2 Float cases evacuated to C.M.V.S.	
	18.9.17		27 Cases evacuated to C.M.V.S. PROVEN. — 36 by Float (2 REMOUNT scouts for retraining)	
			2 Float cases admitted, 20 T.T. 0862. P/A/Corpl. SPINK. SS appointed P/A/Sergt. vice. A.V.C. Local Corps Order. N°90. with effect from 17th inst.	
	19.9.17		17 Cases evacuated to C.M.V.S. - PROVEN. 36 by Float. (2 Remount cases for retraining) 1 Float case admitted. A Special Effective Strength Return Rendered to D.A.D.V.S. in acc with XVIIIth Corps Routine Order N° 676 2 Divn Routine Order N° 705. and approved.	
	20.9.17		8 cases evacuated to C.M.V.S. 1 FLOAT. 1 FLOAT case collected from 511 R.E. Coy.	
	21.9.17		27 " " " " 2 FLOAT. N° 1046. P/A/Sgt. ELLISON. E, dropped to N°3. VET. HOSP in accordance with intimation from O/c Base Records N°7/9 697/17. weekly returns submitted and approved by DADVS.	
	22.9.17		2 FLOAT cases to C.M.V.S. 1 FLOAT case evacuated from 511 RE Coy. AF B213 approved by DADVS	
	23.9.17		22 Animals to C.M.V.S. 1 FLOAT. 1 FLOAT adm from 2/8 LONDON REGT.	
	24.9.17		SE 9389 Pte. Sergeant M. reports for duty on return from leave, 2 FLOAT cases collected.	
	25.9.17		16 Animals to C.M.V.S. 3 FLOAT cases collected	
	26.9.17		T.T. 0689 Pte Thompson H. returns from Rest Camp. 3 FLOAT cases adm. 19 animals to C.M.V.S.	

C W Hunter Capt AVC

Army Form C. 2118.

WAR DIARY
or
INTELLIGENCE SUMMARY

(Erase heading not required.) 2/1 London M.V.S. 58th Division

Place	Date	Hour	Summary of Events and Information	Remarks and references to Appendices
In the field	27/9/17		1 FLOAT case to C.M.V.S. 2 by MOTOR AMB. 1 FLOAT case admitted, weekly returns rendered to D.A.D.V.S. being one day earlier owing to D.H.Q. leaving the area. Returns approved. T.T. 0874 A/L/cpl Cunbush leg recommended for promotion to 9/A/cpl this app awaiting compensation in local Corps Orders	
	28/9/17		29 Animals to C.M.V.S. 2 by FLOAT. 1 FLOAT case admitted, Section jerry attached to 49th Divn.	
	29/9/17		39 Animals to C.M.V.S. 2 by FLOAT. 4 FLOAT cases adm.	
	30/9/17		2 Mules evacuated by FLOAT to C.M.V.S. FLOAT cases adm.	

Capt. Meather Capt.
OC 58th Divn MVS

2449 Wt. W14957/M90 750,000 1/16 J.B.C. & A. Forms/C.2118/12.

WAR DIARY
INTELLIGENCE SUMMARY

2/3rd London M.V.S. 58th Division

Army Form C. 2118.

Place	Date	Hour	Summary of Events and Information	Remarks and references to Appendices
In the Field	1/10/17		15 Animals evacuated to C.M.V.D. 5 Horse cases collected. Horse rugs drawn.	
	2/10/17		49 " " " " " 3 by Float. 36 animals admitted. 2 by float	
	3/10/17		35 " " " " " 2 " , 30 " " 2 by Float	
			1 Float case collected	
	4/10/17		59 Animals evacuated to C.M.V.D. 4 by Float 6 by motor.	
	5/10/17		18 " " " " 3 " 5 Horses to C.M.V.D.	
	6/10/17		In compliance with instructions from 2 Div's V'Army, 4 men detached for duty with C.M.V.D. XIV Corps	
			F.T. 0731 Pte. HEASMAN D. 0757 Pte HOOKE J.	
			0673 Pte. POPKIN J.H. SE 9388. Pte SERJEANT. M.	
			Instructions received via Capt SLOCOCK A.V.C. O.C. XIV C.M.V.D	
	7/10/17		10 Animals evacuated to C.M.V.D. 2 by float. 1 Foot case collected.	
	8/10/17		11 Animals admitted. 32 animals evacuated 2 destroyed	
	9/10/17		54 " "	1 destroyed
	10/10/17		35 " " 60 " "	1 "
	11/10/17		21 " " 2 " "	
	12/10/17		40 " " 70 " "	
	13/10/17		13 " " 1 " "	
	14/10/17		42 " " " "	
	15/10/17		26 " " 30 " "	
	16/10/17		11 (A) men reported from 70 24. Vet Hosp to replace 11(A) men of this section, report on their unsuitability (for riding less) submitted to 500 V.S. gn Div., who inspected them and expressed agreement with report.	

C.H. Sheather Capt.
OC 2/3rd Ldn M.V.S.

WAR DIARY or INTELLIGENCE SUMMARY

Army Form C. 2118.

2/1st LONDON M.V.S. 58 Divn.

Place	Date	Hour	Summary of Events and Information	Remarks and references to Appendices
In the field	16/10/17		16 Animals admitted. 30 Animals evacuated. ADVS XVIII Corps inspected 11(B) men from 24 VET HOSP.	
"	17/10/17		DDVS 1st ARMY inspected & attached stray animals awaiting for issue to REMOUNTS. TT.0646 Pte FURBER F. dispatched to C.M.V.D to relieve SE 9388 Pte Sergeant M. Nearer to run Best	
	18/10/17		TT 0689 Pte THOMPSON H. admitted to XVIII Dressing Station Sick. Weekly Returns rendered to DADVS 9th Divn & approved.	
	19/10/17		DADVS, DDVS, ADVS, DAEVS & MAJ. WADLEY The inspection General inspection of Section by DoJ.V.S being held to ascertain the suitability of 11 P.B men sent to replace 11 Amen from 1024 Vet Hospital. DoJ.V.S gave verbal instructions to send JA men to Base + retain 11PB men on account of the exceptional pressure of work :— TT. 0872 Pte/Cpl McALLAN W. dispatched to No 2 Vet Hospital for further training + examination for appointment as S/SAVE to a field unit.	
	20/10/17		The following men were admitted for Duty at C.M.V.D. SE 2702 Pte M. Govern T. SE 2599 Pte Broughton W. SE 27272. Pte Halforten D. SE 27262. Pte FAWTHORPE. W to Relieve Pte FURBER HEASMAN. HOOKE J. HOPKIN J.H.	
	21/10/17		The following class "A" men were dispatched to No 2 Vet Hospital in acc with compulsory Transfer to combatant units. Pte FURBER. FORD HEASMAN. HOOKE J. HOPKIN J.H. RACKHAM	
	22/10/17		Pte HEASMAN being retained in the Section temporarily as no other cook available.	
	23/10/17		Grooms Pte B.S. Annis to Q.H.G. DADV. Asst/District L.H.Q. Minister, the situation of Improvement A/4 081 Mny 2 B	
	24/10/17		Lt/Ft Blatchley for treatment of Egypt. TT. 0713 Pte Pelham G was dispatched to No 2 Return Hospital Unfit in accordance with instructions, the Christy Vet. Officer.	
	25/10/17		64 Animals taken over from 2/4th Mobile Veterinary Section. 19 Animals admitted of various units; 1 n.c.o 4 men were attached for duty with the Section from 2/6 Batt. Queen's Regt T. Comfy.	

R.R. Purcell. Lieut R.V.C.

Army Form C. 2118.

68 Mob. Vet. Sec.

Vol 10

WAR DIARY
or
INTELLIGENCE SUMMARY
(Erase heading not required.)

Place	Date	Hour	Summary of Events and Information	Remarks and references to Appendices
In the field	26/10/17		Evacuation of 56 animals to Corps M.V.D.	
	" "		T.0707 Pte Willick ♯ N.T. reported for duty from 64 Casualty Clearing Station.	
	27/10/17		Evacuation of 52 animals to Corps M.V.D.	
	28/10/17		Evacuation of 33 animals to 9 Mobile Vet Corps M.V.D.	
	29/10/17		Evacuation of 53 animals to Corps M.V.D.	
	30/10/17		N.8. 26166 Pte Bufford Q.Y. & 25291 Pte Booth R.S. reported at this section for duty and taken on ttn. strength accordingly.	
	30/10/17		Dilution + treatment cases in the ♯ I on V.S.	
	30/10/17		1 W.O. & 7 men returning to 76 London Regiment for duty	
	31/10/17		1 N.C.O. & 3 men joined from 2/4 London Regiment for duty.	
	31/10/17		Routine. Daily quantity returns rendered.	

J.J.B. Lovell
Capt RAVC

WAR DIARY or INTELLIGENCE SUMMARY

Army Form C. 2118

North Vol II

Place	Date	Hour	Summary of Events and Information	Remarks and references to Appendices
Poulina	1-11-17		2 Hor Teams collected from 12th Manchester Regt (Bomb Wala)	
	2-11-17		1 Hor Cart collected from A.B. & Rob R.F.A. (Bomb Wala) 3 Hor Tongas collected 1 from 58 D.A.C. N=2 Sector & 2 from N=3 Sector.	
			1 " mare from Q 291 Bdc. R.F.A.	
	3-11-17		Evacuation to C.M.V.D. Newbrick 40 animals, 39 walking and 1 Hor Team.	
	4-11-17		Daily return rendered to D.A.D.V.S. + approved.	
	5-11-17		1 Hor Team collected from 19th Bty 41st Bde A.F.A.	
			1 Hor Team collected 2 SS mumbling boy R.E. Pbroy Benn Jachment G.S. Wimids.	
	6-11-17		Routine.	
	7-11-17		Evacuation of 60 animals to Newbrick from Poulnick.	
	8-11-17		T.T. 0862 Pte A/S Bgt Squibb O.S. A.V.C. proceeded on 14 days leave to England 8.11.17 to 22.11.17	
	9-11-17		8 Tony mare collected from M.N.P. 58 Division, would go off eye.	
			1 N.C.O. + 5 men joined for duty from 42nd mob V.S. Sect. in accordance with instn. from A.D.V.S. II Corps.	
	10-11-17		Pte 623 P/a/L/Cpl T Buirig. A.V.C. + 11 men joined for duty from 19 Corps M.V.D.	
	11-11-17		Daily Return rendered to D.A.D.V.S. 58 Div.	
			Collection + treatment of cases in action, daily state fur D.A.D.V.S.	
			SE 28049 Pte Pratt G.H. A.V.C. admitted to hospital.	
	12-11-17		Evacuation of 134 animals to hospital, from Cauldron, 1 N.C.O. + 10 men 1/c of team.	
	13-11-17		40 sick obtained.	
	14-11-17		Daily return rendered to D.A.D.V.S. SE 27399 Pte Barkes E. admitted to hospital.	
	15-11-17		Routine Attendance	

WAR DIARY
or
INTELLIGENCE SUMMARY
(Erase heading not required.)

Army Form C. 2118.

Place	Date	Hour	Summary of Events and Information	Remarks and references to Appendices
	16.11.17		Evacuation of 80 hornipeds to Neufchatel from Inoculations IN 6.0 + 10mm 11 reg Ann. 40 mules dispatched	
	17.11.17		The return move to Burns. Mulest E12. D39. Du.T 27	
	18.11.17		Daily DRTs dispatched to D.A.D.V.S. 5-6 Divs.	
	19.11.17		Evacuation to Internat'l conv of 39 horses + 3 Mules	
	20.11.17		Daily State received to 19.01 RVS	
	21.11.17		T.T.0853 L/Cpl PEPE H.H. AVC proceeded with advance party to hum Cues	
	22.11.17		Daily State to DADVS	
	23.11.17		T.T.0862 P/a/sgt SPINKS A.V.C. returned from 14days leave to ENGLAND. 23 annuals evacuated to Base vet Hosp 4 men in charge	
	24.11.17		2.H.B. Loaned to 512 Coy A.S.C. Capt C.J Stoaton	
	25.11.17		Capt C.J. SHEATHER rejoined from special Daily leave to ENGLAND	
	26.11.17		Section moved by road to N.E.P.P.E. halts WIM for night.	
	27.11.17		Capt. E.J.B. SEWELL returned to No.23. VET HOSP for Duty. Section moves to NIELLES-LES-BLEQUIN	
	28.11.17		ROUTINE	
	29.11.17		"	
	30.11.17		Monthly returns rendered to DADVS. & approved. Men paid	

C.J. Sheather Capt.
B.C. 58th Divn M.V.S.

2/1 LONDON. M.V.S. WAR DIARY 58th Divn.
or
INTELLIGENCE SUMMARY

Army Form C. 2118.

Place	Date	Hour	Summary of Events and Information	Remarks and references to Appendices
FIELD.	1.12.17		Routine. 2 Mules admitted. A.F. B213 to HQ 58 DIVN.	
	2.12.17		3 Animals admitted.	
	3.12.17		5 Horses 2 Mules evacuated to St Omer.	
	3.12.17		T.T. 0715. A/Cpl. ROBINSON. E.J. A.M.C. proceed.d. to Divnl. G.A.S. SCHOOL for Course. INCO. 2 Men in charge. T/4/238767. Dr DOBINSON. T.W. Proceeds on leave to ENGLAND. 4.12.17 to 18.12.17. 205046. Dr BROWN. J.E. R.F.A. returned to unit by rail. 200823. Dr BROWN. T.H. returned to unit in charge of officers charge. One animal admitted.	
	4.12.17		1 Float case evacuated. T.T. 0801. Pte/SBGT. OGDEN. W. proceeds to ENGLAND on 15 days balance of furlough.	
	5.12.17		4 Animals evacuated to 23 Vet Hospital. 1 Mule admitted	
	6.12.17		2 Animals evacuated to 23 Vet Hospital by Ambulance.	
	7.12.17		SE 23850 Pte Abrahams. H. 14 days leave to ENGLAND.	
	8.12.17		The Section proceeded to new area, stopping the night at the Pipe.	
	9.12.17		" " arrived at new Area. Sheet 28. A 28 D9K.	
	11.12.17		Took over command of 1st Corps M.V.D. 7 Animals taken over from 405th M.V.S.	
	12.12.17		Daily state rendered to A.D.V.S. 7 Corps. Returns Demands rendered to D.A.D.V.S.	
	13.12.17		DAILY STATE rendered to A.D.V.S. 2 animals admitted.	
	14.12.17		Return for 1914 rendered to D.A.D.V.S.	
	15.12.17		13 animals admitted	
	16.12.17		8 " "	
			12 " "	

C A Bloomers Capt

2/1 LONDON. M.V.S. WAR DIARY or INTELLIGENCE SUMMARY

58th DIVN.

Army Form C. 2118.

Place	Date	Hour	Summary of Events and Information	Remarks and references to Appendices
FIELD.	7.12.17		8 animals evacuated. 1 N.C.O. 18 men in charge. 10 Mules.	
	18.12.17		24 Animals admitted. DAILY STATE to A.D.V.S.	
	19.12.17		9 " " " "	
	20.12.17		10 " " " "	
	21.12.17		10 " " " "	
	22.12.17		68 " " 6 Animals admitted	
	23rd		Evacuated 6 Base.	
			No 7683 Pte MACDONALD.A 13th Labour Coy evacuated to 7th Corps M.V.D. returned to unit. 8 animals admitted	
	24th		9 animals admitted	
			Pte 0801 P/A/15/39F OLDEN. W. returned 9/15 days balance of Furlough to ENGLAND	
			S.E. 26/66. Pte Byford. A. admitted to Hospital	
			No 84.B. Pte TIERNEY. W	
			No SE 8824. Pte MORRIS. W.J. 42" M.V.S. attached 7th Corps. M.V.D. returned to their unit.	
			No S.E. 4611. Pte ATKINSON. R. } 42" M.V.S Joined 7th Corps M.V.D. for duty	
			No S.E. 3097. Pte ROPER. E. }	
			No S.E. 23850. Pte ABRAHAMS. H. returned from 14 days leave to ENGLAND.	
			10 Animals admitted.	
	25th		37 Animals evacuated from Peselhoek. PESELHOEK.	
	26th		" Animals admitted. 1 Float car from B291 R.F.A.	
	27th		17 animals admitted, 7 animals Return to DAVS.	
	28th		Daily State to ADVS.	
	29th		Routine. Cpl. GOMM. W.J. and 8 men returned to 42" MVS. 21 animals taken over from their	
	30th		SE. 6735. Cpl. GOMM. W.J and 3 men returned to 42" MVS.	
	31st		Routine.	
			110 Animals from 58" Divn MVS + 7 from 45 MVS evacuated to NEUFCHATEL. 15 mules. 15 men 1 NCO.	
			6 men accounted for duty from Base to return to their units	
			Thirty by return to D/ADVS. Cash. Account to OC Clearing House, BASE	

E/A Sheppard Capt

WAR DIARY or INTELLIGENCE SUMMARY

2/1 Lond. M V S — 58th Divn. Sheet 2

Army Form C. 2118.

Place	Date	Hour	Summary of Events and Information	Remarks and references to Appendices
FIELD.	1.1.18		Routine.	
	2.1.18		" Weekly returns rendered to D.A.D.V.S.	
	3.1.18		" Inspection of unit by D.V.S & DDVS IV Army.	
	4.1.18		4 men from 45th M.V.S. joined for duty	
	5.1.18		Routine. A.F. B 213 rendered to D.H.Q.	
		7T 0115 91A/Cpl ROBINSON.F.G. proceeded on 14 days leave to ENGLAND.	
	6.1.18		Routine.	
	7.1.18		136 Animals evacuated from PIESELHOEK. 1 NCO & 13 men in charge	
		T.T. 0574. 91A/Cpl. CORBISHLEY. P. AVC. returned from 14 days leave to ENGLAND.	
	8.1.18		T.T. 0858 91E POPE. H.H. admitted to 134 FIELD. AMB. fractured ankle.	
		T 9/23.9224 D" HUMPHREY P.T. A.S.C. 509 By A.S.C. reported for duty	
		Vce EN GLAND T4/123.8767. D" DOBINSON. T.W. A.S.C. adm. Hospital, whilst on leave	
		in ENGLAND.	
	9.1.18		SECTION moves to new area. Map Ref. Sheet 27. 7.30. A.98.	
		63 Animals. 1 mule, 1 NCO, 17 men, 2 HD Horses, 19 S. Waggon & harness	
		handed over to O.C. 45th M.V.S. 33rd DIVN.	
		6 Animals, 2 mules taken over from O.C. 45 M V.S.	
	10.1.18		Routine. Weekly returns to D.A.D.V.S.	
	11.1.18		"	
	12.1.18		"	
	13.1.18		"	
	14.1.18		39 Animals evacuated, 5 hoses, 2 men i/c.	
	15.1.18		Classification of all men & NCOs in Section in an with instructions from D.D.V.S. IV Corps	

C B Westley CAPT.
O.C. 2/1 Lond. M.V.S. 58 Divn.

WAR DIARY or INTELLIGENCE SUMMARY

Army Form C. 2118.

2/1 Lond M.V.S. 58th DIVN. Sheet 7

Place	Date	Hour	Summary of Events and Information	Remarks and references to Appendices
IN THE FIELD	16.1.18		S.E. 1857 A/L Cpl THRESHER B. & Pte BOOTH R.S. A.V.C. proceeded from 78 PERM.V.D.E. with cow chilled ponies to new area.	
	17.1.18		14 Animals evacuated to 7 Corps M.V.D. SIMDE	
	18.1.18		"	
	19.1.18		Weekly Returns to D.A.D.V.S.	
	20.1.18		Routine	
	21.1.18		Classification of NCOs & men rendered to D.A.D.V.S.	
	22.1.18		Section proceeds by road to Railhead & entrains for new area.	
	23.1.18		Arrives at new area. C.O.R. 131/E.	
			T.T. 0758 Sadler HOOKE W. despatched to No 24 VET.HOSP. on instruction from O.I./C BASE RECORDS. A.V.C.	
			S.E. 214.85 Pte CORDES. W. A.V.C. adm. Hospital "Pyrexia"	
	24.1.18		T.T. 0715 R.A. Cpl. ROBINSON. E.G. returned from leave	
	25.1.18		32 Animals 1 mule evacuated to No 7 Vet.Hosp. I.NCO. 4 men w. charge.	
	26.1.18		Weekly returns to D.A.D.V.S.	
			A.F.B. 213 rendered to A.D.A.Q.	
			T.T. 0873. Pte LEWIS. F.C. A.V.C. 14 days leave to ENGLAND.	
	27.1.18		1 NCO & 2 men returned from No7 Vet. Hospital. 2 men remaining there under arrest.	
			2 Animals collected from FRENCH Vet.Stations.	
	28.1.18		2 men arrived from FORGES-LES-EAUX, under escort. SE 27012 Pte McGovern. & SE. 27272 Pte HALLERON. B.	
	29.1.18		Pte McGovern awarded 7 days F.P. No2. Pte HALLERON handed over to R.P.M. awaiting trial.	

C.J. Sheather CAPT.
O.C. 2/1 Lond. M.V.S. 58 Divn.

Army Form C. 2118.

WAR DIARY
or
INTELLIGENCE SUMMARY

2/1 LOND M.V.S. 58th DIVN.

Sheet 3.

Place	Date	Hour	Summary of Events and Information	Remarks and references to Appendices
FIELD	29/11/18		Evacuation to 707 V.A. Hosp. 26 Animals NCO 3 men i/c.	
	30		Routine	
	31		N.C.O. 3 men returning from 707 V.A Hospital. 1 Horse evacuated from 2/Battalion. T.T. 0707 Pte MILLICK F. O. proceed on 14 days leave to ENGLAND.	

C.A. Cheston Capt
O.C. 2/1 Lond. MVS. 58 Divn.

WAR DIARY or **INTELLIGENCE SUMMARY**

Army Form C. 2118.

58th (London) Mtd. Vty. See Vol 14.

Place	Date	Hour	Summary of Events and Information	Remarks and references to Appendices
In the Fd	1/2/18		Routine. 1 Horse collected from French Army, left on issue of march by 14 D.A.C. at ROSIERES.	
do	2/2/18		Routine. 3 cases admitted.	
do	3/2/18		Routine. Pte. McGovern, J. NBC rejoined from 4 P.M. 58 Sqn. SE 27017. Pte. McGovern, J. NBC rejoined from 4 P.M. 58 Sqn.	
do	4/2/18		Evacuation of 21. Animals to FORGES-LES-EAUX from CORBIE. 1 N.C.O. & 2 Gunners in charge.	
do	5/2/18		Section moves to new area at HAMECOURT. leaving CORBIE at 5 a.m. proceeding through DEMUIN. Section halted & watered & fed at 12.45. Left DEMUIN 1.45. Section arrived at BOUCHOIR 4 p.m. & halted for the night: men slept in old ruins, horses picketed out on lines.	
do	6/2/18		Section moves off from BOUCHOIR at 7.45. halted at ROYE. Horses watered & fed, Water carts filled up. Left ROYE at 10.45. arrived at BUSSY 3 p.m. men had a good dinner. Horses picketed on lines.	

C H Bleather Capt

Army Form C. 2118.

WAR DIARY
or
INTELLIGENCE SUMMARY
(Erase heading not required.)

Instructions regarding War Diaries and Intelligence Summaries are contained in F. S. Regs., Part II. and the Staff Manual respectively. Title Pages will be prepared in manuscript.

Place	Date	Hour	Summary of Events and Information	Remarks and references to Appendices
In the Field	9/2/18		Section left Bussy 7.45 am. Horses fed on the line of march. Arrived at DAMPCOURT 12 oclock. M.A.P. Ref. Sheet 7.70. 27 C.2.2. Suitable standing for horses, good billets for men, excellent watering place.	
do	11/2/18		SE 21485. Pte CORDES W. rejoined from 41 Sty Hospital	
do	14/2/18		SE 27186. Pte DOBSON W refunded for duty from No 2 Vety Hosp. T.T.0873. Pte LEWIS P. rejoined off 14 days leave to England.	
do	12/2/18		Formation from APPILLY to FORGES-LES-EAUX of 45 animals 1 NCO r 5 men in charge.	
do	13/2/18		Routine	
do	14/2/18		Routine	
do	15/2/18		SE 25236. Pte CLARK H. A.V.C. returned for duty from 23 Vety Hospital.	
do	16/2/18		Routine	
do	17/2/18		Routine. T.T.0871 Sgton Stuart J. a v.s proceeded on 14 days leave to England.	
do	18/2/18		Routine	

C.F. Sheather Capt.

Army Form C. 2118.

WAR DIARY
or
INTELLIGENCE SUMMARY
(Erase heading not required.)

Instructions regarding War Diaries and Intelligence Summaries are contained in F. S. Regs., Part II. and the Staff Manual respectively. Title Pages will be prepared in manuscript.

Place	Date	Hour	Summary of Events and Information	Remarks and references to Appendices
In the Field	19/2/18		TT.7079 Pte KILLICK J.S. A.V.C. returned off 14 days leave to England. Evacuation of 44 animals to FORGES-LES-EAUX from APPILLY. 1 NCO & 3 MEN i/c. Routine	
do	20/2/18			
do	21/2/18		SE-7373 Pte HALLERON D. A.V.C. proceeded by P.S. P.M.T. via United K. 28 days. Z.P. No 1. 1 NCO & 5 men return from conducting sick horses to Base. 144 animals evacuated to FORGES-LES-EAUX from APPILLY. 1 man 4 NCO i/c	
do	22/2/18			
do	23/2/18		TT.0695 Pte PETCH. E.13. proceeds on 14 days leave to ENGLAND. VIA. BOULOGNE.	
do	24/2/18		TT.1689. Pte THOMPSON. H. A.V.C. admitted to Hospital "N.Y.D." Routine. 1 NCO & 1 man returned from conducting sick horses to Base.	
do	25/2/18			
do	26/2/18		Evacuation of 16 animals to FORGES-LES-EAUX from APPILLY. 1 NCO & 1 man i/c. Routine	
do	27/2/18			
do	28/2/18		Routine. Monthly returns & cash account forwarded.	

C.A.Shratter Capt

Army Form C. 2118.

WAR DIARY
or
INTELLIGENCE SUMMARY

2/1st LOND. M.V.S. 58th DIVN.

(Erase heading not required.)

Place	Date	Hour	Summary of Events and Information	Remarks and references to Appendices
Field.	1/3/18		Evacuation of 11 Animals to No. 7 Vet Hospital. T.T 0689. Pte Thompson H A.V.C. rejoined for duty from Hospital.	Cap5
	2/3/18		Routine.	Cap5
	3/3/18		"	Cap5
	5/3/18		Evacuation to No. 7 Vet Hospital. 16 Animals	Cap5
	6/3/18		T.T. 0765. Pte. Atkinson W. proceeded on 14 days leave to ENGLAND.	Cap5
	7/3/18		1 Stray Mule brought in by C/291 Bde R.F.A 58th Divn. 1 Mule carcase sold to M. HOUSSEAU. 15 Rue de PARIS. NOYON for 120 f[ranc]s for human consumption	Cap5
	8/3/18		Evacuation of 30 Animals to No. 7 Vet Hospital	Cap5
	9/3/18		Routine. Weekly report on Land under cultivation rendered to DA.D.V.S	Cap5
	10/3/18		Routine	Cap5
	11/3/18		"	Cap5
	12/3/18		Evacuation of 17 Animals to No. 7 Vet Hospital	Cap5
	13/3/18		Inspection of Unit by A.D.V.S. IIIrd Corps: T.T. 0695. Pte PETCH.E 13 A.V.C. returned from 14 days leave to ENGLAND. T.T. 0689. Pte THOMPSON. H Ave. proceeded on 14 days leave to ENGLAND.	Cap5
	14/3/18		Pte WATTS. H Ave. joined for duty as IIIrd Corps. SKINNER.	Cap5
	15/3/18		Evacuation of 19 Animals to No. 7 Vet Hospital	Cap5
	16/3/18		Routine.	Cap5
	17/3/18		"	Cap5
	18/3/18		2 Stray horses brought in by No 2 Sect 58th D.A.C.	Cap5

WAR DIARY or INTELLIGENCE SUMMARY

2/1st LOND. M.V.S.   38th DIVN.

Army Form C. 2118.

Place	Date	Hour	Summary of Events and Information	Remarks and references to Appendices
Field	19/3/18		41. Animals evacuated to No 7 Vet. Hospital	C+B
"	20/3/18		Routine Inspection of Section by Major Sire Eaton D.S.V.O. & D.A.D.V.S. 38 Divn.	R.H.
"	21/3/18		Capt E.H. Shrathin A.V.C. proceeded on 14 days leave to England. Weekly Returns rendered to D.A.D.V.S. 58 Divn.	R.H.
"	22/3/18		Evacuation of 17 animals to Forges-Les-Eaux, from Appilly. 1 N.C.O. & 3 men in charge.	R.H.
"	23/3/18		Section moves from Dampcourt to Morlincourt.	R.H.
"	24/3/18		1 N.C.O. & 3 men returned from Base. Evacuation of 13 animals to Forges-Les-Eaux from Noyon.	R.H.
"	25/3/18		Section moves from Morlincourt to Ribecourt.	R.H.
"	26/3/18		Section moves from Ribecourt to Carle Pont. Thence to Nampcel. Horses picquetted on lines, men slept in a dug-out. Routine.	R.H.
"	27/3/18			R.H.
"	28/3/18		Routine. Weekly Returns rendered to D.A.D.V.S. 38 Divn.	R.H.

R.F. Strangeways
W.

NYLAND. M.V.S. 58 DIVN.

Army Form C. 2118.

WAR DIARY
or
INTELLIGENCE SUMMARY

(Erase heading not required.)

Instructions regarding War Diaries and Intelligence
Summaries are contained in F. S. Regs., Part II.
and the Staff Manual respectively. Title Pages
will be prepared in manuscript.

Place	Date	Hour	Summary of Events and Information	Remarks and references to Appendices
Field	29.3.18		Routine.	RH
"	30.3.18		Routine. Capt. R.F. Stirling, A.V.C. took command of this Section temporarily.	RH
	31.3.18		Routine. Cash a/c rendered to. Office cleaning House Base.	RH

Date of Embarkation of this Section
25-1-1917.

R.F. Stirling
Capt. A.V.C.
A/c m/s
58 Divn m/s

Army Form C. 2118.

WAR DIARY
or
INTELLIGENCE SUMMARY
(Erase heading not required.)

71st (London) F.V.S. 58th Division

Instructions regarding War Diaries and Intelligence Summaries are contained in F.S. Regs., Part II. and the Staff Manual respectively. Title Pages will be prepared in manuscript.

Place	Date	Hour	Summary of Events and Information	Remarks and references to Appendices
In the Fd.	1/4/18		Routine	C+S
"	2/4/18		Evacuation of 12 animals to LA MALADRERIE RETHONDES. IN COY 2 men in charge	C+S
"	3/4/18		Routine	C+S
"	4/4/18		Section moves from NAMPCEL to NEUVRAA, marching by road.	C+S
"	5/4/18		to ST. PIERRE IGLE. Halted for the night.	C+S
"	6/4/18		Section proceeds by road to LONGPONT for returning to LONGPRE.	C+S
"			Section debusses at LONGUEAUX & proceeds by road to new site at ROPE FACTORY, SALEUX.	C+S C+S
"	7/4/18		Routine	C+S
"	8/4/18		Routine	C+S
"	8/4/18		770965 Pte ATKINSON.W. & 770669 Pte THOMPSON H returned off 14 days leave to ENGLAND	C+S
"	9/4/18		Evacuation of 10 animals to 185 VETY HOSPITAL ROUEN. 1 man in charge. Capt. C H SHEATHER A.V.C. returned to Section for duty	C+S
"	9/4/18		Capt. R J STIRLING A.V.C. returned to 76 Bde R.F.A. for duty	C+S
"	10/4/18		Evacuation of 20 animals to 14 VETY HOSPITAL ABBEVILLE 2 men in charge	C+S

C J Sheather Capt.

Army Form C. 2118.

2/2 London Fd. A. L.   5 Division

WAR DIARY
or
INTELLIGENCE SUMMARY
(Erase heading not required.)

Instructions regarding War Diaries and Intelligence Summaries are contained in F. S. Regs., Part II. and the Staff Manual respectively. Title Pages will be prepared in manuscript.

Place	Date	Hour	Summary of Events and Information	Remarks and references to Appendices
In the Field	11/4/18		Routine. Freshly Rations received to D.A.D.V.S. & Div.	Co/S
"	12/4/18		Evacuation of 67 animals to South Army V.E.S. PICAVIGNY. 4 N.C.Os & 8 men in charge. 1 animal conveyed by Motor Ambulance.	Co/S
"	13/4/18		Evacuation of 24 animals to South Army V.E.S. PICAVIGNY. 1 N.C.O & 3 men in charge. 2 animals conveyed by Ambulance.	Co/S
"	14/4/18		Evacuation of 14 animals to South Army V.E.S. PICAVIGNY. 1 N.C.O & 2 men in charge.	Co/S
"	15/4/18		Evacuation of 8 animals to V.E.S. PICAVIGNY.	Co/S
"	16/4/18		1 animal conveyed by Ambulance to V.E.S. PICAVIGNY. 1 N.C.O & 2 men in charge.	Co/S
"	"		5 men joined from No 5 VETY HOSP. ABBEVILLE.	Co/S
"	17/4/18		Evacuation of 15 animals to South Army V.E.S. PICAVIGNY.	Co/S
"	18/4/18		Evacuation of 11 animals to South Army V.E.S. PICAVIGNY. 1 Reat-case & 4 Horses.	Co/S
"	19/4/18		Inspection of Section by the D.V.S. & Lt. Col. Mc Gowan. Evacuation of 24 Animals to V.E.S. PICAVIGNY.	Co/S
"	20/4/18		Routine.	Co/S
"	21/4/18		Evacuation of 24 animals to No 15 VETY HOSP ROUEN. 2 men in charge.	Co/S
"	22/4/18		Evacuation of 18 animals to No 15 VETY HOSP ROUEN. 2 men in charge.	Co/S

Co/s Commander

Army Form C. 2118.

WAR DIARY
or
INTELLIGENCE SUMMARY

(Erase heading not required.)

Ꮽ/ЈА (ʀoaԃ) ʍ.V.S.   58 Division

Instructions regarding War Diaries and Intelligence Summaries are contained in F. S. Regs., Part II and the Staff Manual respectively. Title Pages will be prepared in manuscript.

Place	Date	Hour	Summary of Events and Information	Remarks and references to Appendices
In the Fd	22/4/18		SE27272 Pte HALLERON.D A.V.C. & SE27012 Pte McGOVERN J A.V.C. despatched to No 2 VETY HOSP. under-vet. instructions from the D.V.S. Evacuation of 18 animals to No 15 VETY HOSP. ROUEN. 18 Hides forwarded.	CoS
"	23/4/18		Routine.	CoS
"	24/4/18		Evacuation of 30 animals to No 15 Vety Hosp. ROUEN. & Hides forwarded. 2 men in charge.	CoS
"	25/4/18		SE9725 Pte EVANS. A. A.V.C. & SE16723 Pte THOMPSON W. A.V.C. joined for duty from No 14 VETY HOSP ABBEVILLE. Evacuation of 7 animals to South Army V.E.S. POAVIGNY. 2 Hides forwarded. 1 N.C.O & 2 men in charge.	CoS
"	26/4/18		Evacuation of 2 animals to 30 M.V.S. 18 Division.	CoS
"	27/4/18		Evacuation of 11 animals to South Army V.E.S. PICAVIGNY. 8 Hides forwarded. 1 N.C.O. & 3 men in charge.	CoS
"	28/4/18		Section by route to MAN SECT. for the night.	CoS
"	29/4/18		Section moves off & arrives at New Site allocated at NEUVILLE at 4 p.m. Monthly Returns rendered to D.A.D.V.S.	CoS
	30/4/18			CoS

C.J. Sleventor Capt DV

WAR DIARY
or
INTELLIGENCE SUMMARY

Army Form C. 2118.

(Erase heading not required.)

Place	Date	Hour	Summary of Events and Information	Remarks and references to Appendices
NEUVILLE	1.5.18		Routine, weekly Returns rendered to D.A.D.V.S. 58. Div.	A.C.
	2.5.18		"	A.C.
	3.5.18		Evacuation of 27 animals to No 14 Vety Hospital Abbeville.	A.C.
	4.5.18		5 Privates A.V.C. returned to No. 5 Vety Hospital, instructions A D V S III Corps.	A.C.
			Evacuation of 29 animals to No 14 Vety Hospital Abbeville	A.C.
	5.5.18		S.E 2566 86 Pte Dobson 1st A.V.C. despatched to III Corps V.E.S.	A.C.
			Capt. D. Campbell A.V.C. proceed on leave for duty	A.C.
			Section moved to new area by road. - Killed the night at Hangest.	A.C.
	6.5.18		Section moved off at 9.A.M. arriving at Pumiott at 6. P.M.	A.C.
HANGEST	7.5.18		Capt. E. H. Shealter A.V.C. TT 0871 Pte Lewis P. L. A.V.C. transferred 63rd V.E.S. III Corps.	A.C.
Pt.ERRECQ	8.5.18		Weekly Returns rendered to D.A.D.V.S. 58. Div.	A.C.
	9.5.18		Evacuation to Aust V.E.S. at "Clemont" Chateau of 9 animals 1 H.C.O. 3 men in charge.	A.C.
	10.5.18		Routine	A.C.
	11.5.18		Forage & remounts returns rendered to D.A D.V.S.	A.C.
	12.5.18		S.E. 9727 Pte Evans a admitted to 2/2 H.C. V.Amb. N.Y.D.	A.C.
	13.5.18		Evacuation to Aust V.E.S. "Clemont" Chateau of 21 animals 1 N.C.O. 3 men in charge to No 5 Vety Hospital Base.	A.C.
	14.5.18		S.E 3106 PTE WARD. C. A.V.C. despatched to A.D.V.S. III Corps.	A.C.
	15.5.18		Inspection of Section by A.D.V.S. III Corps.	A.C.

D Campbell Capt

WAR DIARY or INTELLIGENCE SUMMARY

Army Form C. 2118.

(Erase heading not required.)

Place	Date	Hour	Summary of Events and Information	Remarks and references to Appendices
PIERREGOT	16.5.18		Weekly returns furnished to D.A.D.V.S. 68 Div.	
			4 Animals evacuated to Aust V.E.S. Orincourt Chateau. 1 N.C.O. & 2 men in charge.	
	17.5.18		Section moves to new area Donfay SE 27262. Pte Vaultopu w.e.f SE 29599 Pte Bringhim W. despatched to XIX Corps V.E.S. Pequnry for duty	
DONFAY	18.5.18		Routine	
	19.5.18		Routine	
	20.5.18		Evacuation of 2 horses & 1 foal to N.O. VII V.E.S. 1 N.C.O. & 3 men in charge.	
	21.5.18		" " 11 animals " " " 1 " 3 " "	
	22.5.18		Routine	
	23.5.18		Evacuation of 4 animals to VII Aust V.E.S. 1 " 2 " "	
	24.5.18		" of 13 " " " " 1 " 4 " "	
	25.5.18		Routine	
	26.5.18		Evacuation of 2 animals to VII Aust V.E.S.	
	27.5.18		3 Mules & Broken killed by enemy shell fire. 10 injured.	
	28.5.18		Evacuation of 17 animals to VIII Aust- V.E.S. 1 N.C.O. 3 men in charge.	
	29.5.18		" " 1 " " " " by float. 1 Rate forwarded.	
	30.5.18		" " 13 " " " " " "	
	31.5.18		" " 11 " " " " in weekly returns furnished to S.A.A.D.S.	
	31.5.18		Monthly cash account to Brigade Clearing House Base	

J. Campbell Capt

WAR DIARY

7/1 (London) Mob. Vety. Sect. 58 Division

Instructions regarding War Diaries and Intelligence Summaries are contained in F.S. Regs., Part II. and the Staff Manual respectively. Title pages will be prepared in manuscript.

Army Form C. 2118.

MOBILE VET'Y. SECTION — 58th LOND. DIVN.

INTELLIGENCE SUMMARY
(Erase heading not required.)

Place	Date	Hour	Summary of Events and Information	Remarks and references to Appendices
CONTAY.	1/7/18		Evacuation of 6 animals to No VII V.E.S. Oincourt Chateau. A.F. B213 rendered to O.R.O. 58 Divn.	DC
— do —	2/7/18		Evacuation of 16 animals to No VII V.E.S. Oincourt Chateau. I N.C.O. & 6 men in charge. One phot. case.	DC
— do —	3/7/18		Under instructions from O/C No VII V.E.S. 58 Divn. T.T.O. & 01 Regt. S/Sgt. ALDEN W. as transferred to No 3 P.E. S. EAU COURT-SUR-SOMME.	DC
— do —	4/7/18		Evacuation of 6 animals to No VII V.E.S. Oincourt Chateau. I N.C.O. & 2 men in charge.	DC
— do —	5/7/18		Routine 1 stray animal admitted to M.V.S.	DC
— do —	6/7/18		Evacuation of 7 animals to No VII V.E.S. Oincourt Chateau. 1 N.C.O. & 4 men in charge. 1 phot. case.	DC
— do —	7/7/18		Evacuation of 2 animals to No VII V.E.S. Oincourt Chateau. 1 Horse formerly 2 men in charge.	DC
— do —	8/7/18		Evacuation 10 animals to No VII V.E.S. Oincourt Chateau. I N.C.O. & 3 men in charge. A.F. B213 rendered to L.H.Q. 58 Divn. Section moves to new site at REINNEVILLE.	DC
REINNEVILLE.	9/7/18		Evacuation of 7 animals to Oincourt Chateau No VII V.E.S. 2 stray animals admitted to M.V.S. SE 21343 F.E.	DC
— do —	10/7/18		WATTS H.A.V.C. returned to Hilgartes W. orders for duty.	DC

D. Campbell
O/C. 58 London M. V. Section

71st (London) Mr. V.S. WAR DIARY 58 Division

Instructions regarding War Diaries and Intelligence Summaries are contained in F.S. Regs. Part II. and the Staff Manual respectively. Title pages will be prepared in manuscript.

Army Form C. 2118.

INTELLIGENCE SUMMARY
(Erase heading not required.)

[Stamp: MOBILE VET:Y Nº 1 SECTION * 58th LOND. DIVISION]

Place	Date	Hour	Summary of Events and Information	Remarks and references to Appendices
REINNEVILLE	10/6/18		Section moves to new area at BREILLY.	AC
BREILLY	11-6-18		Establish Routine Collection & treatment of cases.	AC
do	12.6.18		Evacuation of 5 animals to 19. V.E.S. PICAUIGNY, 1 Float base. 1 N.C.O. & 4 men in charge.	AC
do	13.6.18		Weekly Returns rendered to D.A.D.V.S. 58 Div. Evacuation of 2 animals to 19. V.E.S. PICAUIGNY. 1 N.C.O. 1 man in charge. Collection & treatment of cases.	AC
do	14.6.18		Routine.	AC
do	15.6.18		A.D.B 213 rendered to H.Q.58 Div. Routine	AC
do	16.6.18		Float base collected from 58 Mr. L. Corps.	AC
do	17.6.18		Evacuation of 2 animals to 19 V.E.S. PICAUIGNY. Billetting certificate issued for the period in BREILLY.	AC
do	18.6.18		Section moves to new area by road moving off at 8 am. - arriving about 3pm at new area BEAUCOURT. Map. Ref. 729. A.S.2. 57 L. SE71343. The WATTS H. & V.C. joined from III Corps Hygiene, as trained skinner to Division. Routine. Collection of Horse Hides, Lamb sences etc.	AC
BEAUCOURT	19/6/18		Weekly Returns rendered to D.A.D.V.S. 58 Div.	AC
"	20/6/18			AC

D. Campbell
Lieut. A.V.C.

6.6.18 58 Div Mr. V. Section

21st (London) Sub Vety. Section WAR DIARY 58th Division.

Instructions regarding War Diaries and Intelligence Summaries are contained in F.S. Regs., Part II. and the Staff Manual respectively. Title pages will be prepared in manuscript.

INTELLIGENCE SUMMARY.
(Erase heading not required.)

Place	Date	Hour	Summary of Events and Information	Remarks and references to Appendices
BEAUCOURT	21/6/18		No. 54-2060 Pte. WILD. W 807 taken Evy. att. for duty, proceeds on 14 days leave to ENGLAND.	A
do	22/6/18.		Evacuation of 29 animals to No VII V.E.S. OZINCOURT CHATEAU. 1 N.C.O. 6 men in charge.	do
do	23/6/18		Routine. 1 animal destroyed by Shot. 13 kicks formed.	do
do	24/6/18.		Evacuation of 2 animals to No VII V.E.S. OZINCOURT CHATEAU. Collection & treatment of cases ie M.V.S.	do
do	25/6/18		Evacuation of 19 animals to No VII V.E.S. OZINCOURT CHATEAU. 1 N.C.O. & 2 men in charge.	do
do	26/6/18		Evacuation of 11 animals to No VII V.E.S. OZINCOURT CHATEAU. 1 N.C.O & 2 men in charge. Weekly Returns rendered.	do
do	27/6/18		Evacuation of 33 animals to No VII V.E.S. OZINCOURT CHATEAU. 1 case destroyed by Shot. 1 Horse foundered.	do
do	28/6/18		Evacuation of 16 animals to No VII V.E.S. OZINCOURT CHATEAU. 1 case conveyed by Float. 1 N.C.O. & 4 men in charge. Inspection of Section by Major General. F.W RAMSAY, C.M.G. D.S.O. Commanding 58th (London) Division.	do
do	29/6/18		Evacuation of 16 animals to No VII V.E.S. OZINCOURT CHATEAU.	do
do	30/6/18		Evacuation to No VII V.E.S. OZINCOURT CHATEAU 6: 2 cases i/c C.L. 58 Brand M.V.S. Capt. A.V.C.	
do	"		1 case received to V/6 Clearing Horse Base.	do

77/21 (LONDON) MOBILE VETY. SECT. WAR DIARY 58th DIVISION

Army Form C. 2118.

Instructions regarding War Diaries and Intelligence Summaries are contained in F. S. Regs., Part II. and the Staff Manual respectively. Title pages will be prepared in manuscript.

INTELLIGENCE SUMMARY
(Erase heading not required.)

MOBILE VETY. SECTION — 1 JUL 1918 — 58th LOND. DIVISION

Place	Date	Hour	Summary of Events and Information	Remarks and references to Appendices
BEAUVOIR	1.7.18		Evacuation of 17 Animals to No VII V.E.S. OLINCOURT CHATEAU. 1 N.C.O. + 2 men in charge.	DC
do	2.7.18		Evacuation of 11 animals to No VII V.E.S. OLINCOURT CHATEAU. 1 N.C.O. + 2 men in charge.	DC
do	3.7.18		Evacuation of 10 animals to No VII V.E.S. OLINCOURT CHATEAU. 1 N.C.O. + 4 men in charge. 1 animal arrived by float. Weekly Returns rendered to H. & D. V. & 58 Division.	DC
do	4.7.18		Evacuation of 23 animals to No VII V.E.S. OLINCOURT CHATEAU. 1 N.C.O. + 5 men in charge. Routine & Stray Horses with Traffic Control 58 Divn.	DC
do	5.7.18			DC
do	6.7.18		Evacuation of 30 animals to No VII V.E.S. OLINCOURT CHATEAU. 1 N.C.O. + 7 men in charge. A.T.B213 rendered to H.Q. 58 Divn. Routine & Stray Horses claimed & handed over to Royal Canadian Horse Aly.	DC
do	7.7.18			DC
do	8.7.18		Evacuation of three animals to No VII V.E.S. OLINCOURT CHATEAU; 1 animal conveyed by float. 3 Horses forwarded, 3 men in charge.	DC
do	9.7.18		Evacuation of 19 Animals to No VII V.E.S. OLINCOURT CHATEAU. 1 N.C.O. + 3 men in charge.	DC
do	10.7.18		Evacuation of 26 animals to No VII V.E.S. OLINCOURT CHATEAU. Sub/C. T/E W.I.D. W. (attached for duty) returned off 14 days leave to ENGLAND.	DC

S Campbell
Lt/C 2nd Lond MVS

47 of LONDON. M.V.S. 58 Division.

WAR DIARY
or
INTELLIGENCE SUMMARY

Army Form C. 2118.

MOBILE VET. SECTION
Date 1 JUL 1918
58th LOND. DIVISION

Place	Date	Hour	Summary of Events and Information	Remarks and references to Appendices
BEAUCOURT	11.7.18		Evacuation of 16 animals to VII V.E.S. OZINCOURT. CHATEAU. 1 N.C.O. & 7 men in charge.	DC
do.	12.7.18		Stably Returns rendered to D.A.Q.M.G. 58 DVN. Routine Inspection of Horses lines by D.V.O. 1/3 & 2/3 M.V.S. Field Ambulance.	DC
do.	13.7.18		Evacuation of 13 animals to No VII V.E.S. OZINCOURT CHATEAU. 1 N.C.O. & 3 men in charge.	DC
do.	14.7.18		Evacuation of 23 animals to No VII V.E.S. OZINCOURT CHATEAU. 1 N.C.O. & 4 men in charge.	DC
do.	14.7.18		SE 23850 Pte (A/CPL) ABRAHAMS. H. A.V.C. reported for duty from 58 Mod. Vim. Bath.	DC
do.	15.7.18		Evacuation of 27 animals to No VII V.E.S. OZINCOURT CHATEAU. 1 N.C.O. & 4 men in charge.	DC
do.	"		No 316725 Dr. SCOTTER. T. 3/3 SCOTTISH HORSE att. for duty. Enrolled 14 days leave to ENGLAND. 16/7 to 30/7/18.	DC
do.	16.7.18		Evacuation of 14 animals to No VII V.E.S. OZINCOURT.CHATEAU. 1 man in change by FLOAT. 1 N.C.O. & 4 men in charge.	DC
do.	17.7.18		Evacuation of 10 animals to No VII V.E.S. OZINCOURT CHATEAU. 1 N.C.O. & 2 men in charge.	DC

D. Campbell Capt R.a.V.C.
O.C. 58 Divnl M.V.S.

WAR DIARY 2/1(London) M.V.S. 58 DIVISION.

or

INTELLIGENCE SUMMARY

(Erase heading not required)

Army Form C. 2118.

MOBILE VETY. SECTION
Date 31 JUL 1918
58th LOND. DIVN.

Place	Date	Hour	Summary of Events and Information	Remarks and references to Appendices
BEAUCOURT.	18.7.18.		Weekly Returns rendered to D.A.D.V.S. 58 Div. Lt. HUMPHREYS P.J. A.S.C. proceeds on 14 days leave.	
"	19.7.18		W/5,33,234 to ENGLAND. 20/7/18 to 3/8/18. 1 Medical case collected. Evacuation of 11 animals to VII V.E.S. OLINCOURT. CHATEAU. 1 N.C.O. & 2 men in charge.	
"	20.7.18		Routine. Evacuation of 12 animals to No VII V.E.S. OLINCOURT. CHATEAU. 1 N.C.O. & 2 men in charge. A.P. B.113. returned to D.A.D.V.S.	
"	21.7.18		Routine, collection & treatment of cases.	
"	22.7.18		Evacuation of 13 animals to No VII V.E.S. OLINCOURT. CHATEAU. 1 N.C.O. & 3 men in charge, 1 animal conveyed by ambulance. Evacuation of 21 animals to VII V.E.S. OLINCOURT CHATEAU.	
"	23.7.18		1 N.C.O. & 3 men in charge.	
"	24.7.18		Mobile routine, collection & treatment of cases.	
"	25.7.18		Weekly Returns rendered to D.A.D.V.S.	
"	27.7.18		Routine, collection & treatment of cases.	
"	29.7.18		Evacuation of 17 animals to No VII V.E.S. OLINCOURT CHATEAU. 1 N.C.O. & 3 men in charge. Inspection of station by Col. Campbell D.D.V.S. 3rd Army.	

WAR DIARY
or
INTELLIGENCE SUMMARY

(Erase heading not required.)

Army Form C. 2118.

58th (LONDON) M.V.S.   58 Division

Instructions regarding War Diaries and Intelligence Summaries are contained in F. S. Regs., Part II. and the Staff Manual respectively. Title pages will be prepared in manuscript.

Place	Date	Hour	Summary of Events and Information	Remarks and references to Appendices
BEAUCOURT	28.7.18		Routine. Collection & Sentimed. of cases	
"	29.7.18		Routine. Inspection of cases in No. V.S. by O.C. 58 V.S. 58 Div.	
"	30.7.18		Evacuation of 18 animals to No VII V.E.S. O/INCOURT CHATEAU. 1 N.C.O. & 4 Men in charge. 1 animal conveyed by Float. 2 Hides forwarded.	
"	31.7.18		Evacuation of 1 animal (by Ambulance) to No VII V.E.S. OLINCOURT CHATEAU. 1 N.C.O. in charge. Monthly Returns rendered to D.A.V.S. 58 Div. Cash account to life. Cleaning Stores, Base. SS. 25791 Pte. Booth R.S. A.V.C. proceeds on 14 days leave to ENGLAND. (1/8/18 to 15/8/18.)	

J Campbell Capt. A.V.C.
O.C. 58 Divnl. Mob. Vet. Sec.

217th LOND. MOB. VETY. SECTION.   5th DIVISION.

Army Form C. 2118.

WAR DIARY
or
INTELLIGENCE SUMMARY.
(Erase heading not required.)

Instructions regarding War Diaries and Intelligence Summaries are contained in F.S. Regs., Part II. and the Staff Manual respectively. Title pages will be prepared in manuscript.

Place	Date	Hour	Summary of Events and Information	Remarks and references to Appendices
BEAUCOURT	1-8-18		Weekly Returns rendered to D.A.D.V.S. 5th Divn. Evacuation of 11 animals to No VII V.E.S. Wincourt Chateau. 1 N.C.O. & 7 men in charge. 1 animal conveyed by float. Routine.	LC
"	2-8-18		1 N.C.O. & 7 men in charge.	LC
"	3-8-18		SE19126 B.E. CROSSLAND. H.A.V.C. proceeds on 14 days leave to England at 8.18 6-18 8/8. Evacuation of 5 animals to No VII V.E.S. Wincourt Chateau.	LC
"	4-8-18		1 N.C.O. & 2 men ⟨⟩ charge.	LC
"	"		Station moves from Beaucourt to Vigna Court, moving station at 2.30 p.m. Starting for horses, stalls for ⟨⟩,	DC
"	"		No 316075 Spr. SOUTER. T. 32. Footrot House. returns off 14 days leave to ENGLAND.	DC
"	"		Routine	DC
VIGNACOURT	5-8-18		Evacuation of 3 animals to No VII V.E.S. Wincourt Chateau. 1 N.C.O. & 1 man ⟨⟩ charge.	DC
"	6-8-18		Routine.	DC
"	7-8-18		Evacuation of 1 animal to No VII V.E.S. Wincourt Chateau.	DC
"	8-8-18		Station moves from Vignacourt to Bonnay, the R. service, with out forst. at Bonnay. 1 N.C.O. & 2 men stationed at out forst. Weekly Returns rendered to D.A.D.V.S. 5th Divn. Sgt. Humphreys. Pvt. A.S.C. returned off 14 days leave.	DC

Campbell
Capt A.V.C.
O.C. 217 Div. Mob. Vety. Section.

7/2 LONDON MOB. VETY SECTION.   58 DIVISION.

Army Form C. 2118.

WAR DIARY
or
INTELLIGENCE SUMMARY.

(Erase heading not required.)

Instructions regarding War Diaries and Intelligence Summaries are contained in F. S. Regs., Part II. and the Staff Manual respectively. Title pages will be prepared in manuscript.

Stamp: MOBILE VETY. SECTION / 31 AUG 1918 / 7/2 LOND

Place	Date	Hour	Summary of Events and Information	Remarks and references to Appendices
QUERRIEU	9.8.18		Col. Robinson, A.D.V.S. + 1 man ord. out, on patrol duty on forward area. Good Wagon Lines. To bring in Sick. Weary + wounded Horses.	A.C.
"	10.8.18		C.Q.M.S. received to D.H.Q.	A.C.
"	11.8.18		Evacuation of 17 animals to No VII. V.E.S. ALINCOURT CHATEAU. N.C.O. + 3 men in charge.	A.C.
"	12.8.18		Evacuation of 14 animals to No 3. V.E.S. ALINCOURT CHATEAU. 1 N.C.O. + 2 men in charge.	A.C.
"	13.8.18		Evacuation of 13 animals to No 3 V.E.S. ALINCOURT CHATEAU. 1 N.C.O. + 2 men in charge. St 23235 Pte BATLEY A.V.C. proceeds, on 14 days leave to ENGLAND. (13/8/18 to 27/8/18).	A.C.
"	14.8.18		Evacuation of 7 animals to No 3. V.E.S. ALINCOURT CHATEAU. 1 N.C.O. + 2 men in charge. Nobly Returns received 6-R.A.F.25. 58 Divn. Artillery Trs. 1st 7 Bomar.Y turned over to 2/7 LOND. M.V.S. 47 Divnrs. 1 animal handed over, to 47 Divn. Trs. V.S.	A.C.
"	15.8.18		2 animals evacuated by that to 1st Aust. V.E.S. CORBIE. General Inspection of unit by the A.D of V.S. 4th Aust Divn.	A.C.
"	16.8.18		Evacuation of 7 animals to No 3. V.E.S. ALINCOURT CHATEAU. 2 animals conveyed by ambulance to 1/2 Aust. V.E.S. CORBIE.	A.C.

H. Campbell Lieut
O.C. 58 Divn. Mob. Vety. Sectn

HOLLAND. M.V.S. 58 Division.

WAR DIARY
or
INTELLIGENCE SUMMARY.

Army Form C. 2118.

(Erase heading not required.)

Instructions regarding War Diaries and Intelligence Summaries are contained in F. S. Regs., Part II. and the Staff Manual respectively. Title pages will be prepared in manuscript.

Place	Date	Hour	Summary of Events and Information	Remarks and references to Appendices
QUERRIEU	16.8.18		Inspection of Section by General F.W. Ramsay C.M.G. D.S.O. Commanding 58th Division.	AC
do.	17.8.18.		Evacuation of 7 animals to No 3. V.E.S. VINCOURT CHATEAU. 1 N.C.O & 5 men in charge.	AC
do.	"		3 ambulance cases conveyed to 1st aid. V.E.S. CORBIE. SE25291 Pte BOOTH. R.S. A.V.C. Returned to duty. Off 14 days leave to England.	AC
do.	18/8/18.		SE6678 Pte SIMMONS.T. a.v.c. Proceeds on 14 days leave to England (20/8 to 3/9/18). Routine. 2 Stray animals admitted.	AC
do.	19/8/18.		Inspection of Section by Lt. Col. J. McGowan A.V.C. A.D.V.S. II Corps.A.C	AC
do.	20/8/18.		Routine SE19621 Pte CROSSLAND. H. A.V.C. returned off 14 days leave to England.	AC
do.	21/8/18.		Routine.	AC
do.	22/8/18.		Ruby Retrieve removed to D.A.D.V.S. 58th Division. SE2261S Pte SPEARS. J. a.v.c. T joined for duty from No 2. L.H.D. Base.	AC
do.	23/8/18.		SE27023 Pte FOX V.C. A.V.C. Proceeds on 14 days leave to ENGLAND	AC

J. Campbell Capt. A.V.C.
O.C. 58 Divisional Mob. Vety Section.

WAR DIARY
INTELLIGENCE SUMMARY

2/1st (London) M.V.S. 38 Division.

Army Form C. 2118.

Place	Date	Hour	Summary of Events and Information	Remarks and references to Appendices
QUERRIEU	24.8.18		Evacuation of 9 animals to No.3 V.E.S. CORDY - CHATEAU. 1 N.C.O. & 2 men in charge. 1 animal conveyed by Ambulance to No.1 Aust. V.E.S. at CORBIE.	DC
"	"		Lt. T. O. 9765 H.E. ATKINSON M. A.V.C. despatched to No.2 Vety. Hosp. Base for Medical Inspection & transfer to Infantry if fit.	DC
"	25.8.18		Below moves to new area at HEILLY arriving at 8pm.	
HEILLY	26.8.18		Evacuation of 11 animals to 1st Aust. V.E.S. at CORBIE. 1 N.C.O. & 3 men in charge.	DC
"			Inspection of Return by Col. Tatam D.A.D. V.S. 3rd Army H.Q. Lt. Col.) the Gunner D.D.V.S. 4th Army H.Q. Lt. W. Lt. Col.	DC
"	27.8.18		Return carried from HEILLY to new area at MORLANCOURT. Horses in lines, men in Bivy-acks.	DC
MORLANCOURT	28.8.18		Evacuation of 7 animals to 1st Aust V.E.S. at CORBIE. 1 N.C.O. & 3 men in charge.	DC
"	29.8.18		Weekly Returns rendered to D.A.D.V.S. 58 Division.	DC
"	31.8.18		1 animal conveyed by Ambulance	DC

J. Campbell Capt. A.V.C.
O.C. 2/1st Lond. Mob. Vety. Section

271st (LONDON) M.V.S. 58th Division

WAR DIARY
or
INTELLIGENCE SUMMARY
(Erase heading not required.)

Instructions regarding War Diaries and Intelligence Summaries are contained in F. S. Regs., Part II. and the Staff Manual respectively. Title pages will be prepared in manuscript.

Army Form C. 2118.

MOBILE VET'y SECTION
31 AUG 1918
58th LOND. DIVISION

Place	Date	Hour	Summary of Events and Information	Remarks and references to Appendices
MORLANCOURT	30.8.18		Evacuation of 18 animals to No 3 V.E.S. RIBEMONT 1 N.C.O. & 3 men in charge.	
do	"		Evacuation of 14 animals to No 3. V.E.S. RIBEMONT. 1 N.C.O. & 2 men in charge. 2 animals evacuated by Ambulance. No. 23735 Pte. BATZEY R.C. A.V.C. returned off 14 days leave to ENGLAND.	D.C.
do	31/8/18		Evacuation of 11 animals to No 3. V.E.S. RIBEMONT. 1 N.C.O. & 1 men in charge.	
do	"		Section moved to new area at BRENTAY FARM arriving at new site viâ 10.15 am. Monthly Returns rendered to D.A.D.V.S. 58 Divn, Cash account rendered to 63rd Clearing Horse Base.	D.C.

D Campbell Capt. A.V.C.
O.C. 63 Mobl. Vy. S.

14/7/2 (LONDON) M.V.S.   58th Division

WAR DIARY
or
INTELLIGENCE SUMMARY

(Erase heading not required.)

Place	Date	Hour	Summary of Events and Information	Remarks and references to Appendices
BRONFAY FARM	1/9/18		Evacuation of 13 animals to No 3 V.E.S. at HEILLY 1 N.C.O. + 3 men in charge. 1 animal conveyed by Float.	DC
do	2/9/18		Evacuation of 23 animals to No 3 V.E.S. at BERNANCOURT. 1 N.C.O. + 4 men in charge.	DC
do	3/9/18		Evacuation of 14 animals to No 3 V.E.S. VILLE-SUR-ANCRE. 1 N.C.O. 3 men in charge	DC
do	4/9/18		Evacuation of 30 animals to 3 V.E.S. VILLE-SUR-ANCRE. 1 N.C.O. + 5 men in charge.	DC
do	5/9/18		Evacuation of 70 animals to No 3 V.E.S. VILLE-SUR-ANCRE. 1 N.C.O. + 3 men in charge. Weekly Returns rendered to D.A.D.V.S. 58 Division.	DC
do	6/9/18		Evacuation of 1 animal by Float to No 3 V.E.S. VILLE-SUR-ANCRE.	DC
do	7/9/18		T.T. 0917 Flagstf. Devel.: E.A.&C. proceeds on 14 days leave to England (7/9/18 - 21/9/18) Lt. J. BATES returned to H.Q. 58 Division.	DC
do	8/9/18		Evacuation of 4 animals to No 3 V.E.S. VILLE-SUR-ANCRE.	DC
do	9/9/18		Section moves from BRONFAY FARM to new area at C20.c central south of BOUCHAVESNES.	DC

J. Campbell
O.C. 27 Lond [?] 58 Div

WAR DIARY
INTELLIGENCE SUMMARY

37½ (LONDON) M.V.S. 58 Division. Army Form C. 2118.

Place	Date	Hour	Summary of Events and Information	Remarks and references to Appendices
BOUCHAVESNES	8/9/18		Inspection of unit by A.D.V.S. III Corps & D.A.D.V.S. 58 Division. Evacuation of 2 animals to No. 3 V.E.S. CARNOY.	do
do.	9/9/18		Routine.	do
do.	10/9/18		SE. 27023 Pte. FOX. V.C. returned off 14 days leave to England.	do
do.	11/9/18		Evacuation of 1 animal by float to No 3 V.E.S. CARNOY.	do
do.	12/9/18		Routine.	do
do.	13/9/18		Sgt. 9388 Pte Sargeant. H. A.V.C. granted 14 days leave to England. (14 7/8 6. 28 7/8.) Evacuation of 46 animals to - No. 3. V.E.S. CARNOY. 1 N.C.O. & 6 men in charge.	do
do.	12/9/18		Routine.	do
do.	14/9/18		Evacuation 78 animals to No 3 V.E.S. CARNOY. 1 animal conveyed by float. 1 N.C.O. & 4 men in charge.	do
do.	15/9/18.		Evacuation of 21 Horses to No 3. V.E.S. CARNOY. 1 N.C.O. & 3 men in charge.	do
do.	16/9/18.		Evacuation of 21 animals to No 3. V.E.S. CARNOY. 1 N.C.O. 3 men in charge.	do

J Campbell Capt.
O.C. 2/1 Lond. M V S 58 Divn

WAR DIARY or INTELLIGENCE SUMMARY

2/9 (LOND) M.V.S.   5 8 Division   Army Form C. 2118

Place	Date	Hour	Summary of Events and Information	Remarks and references to Appendices
BOUCHAVESNES	17/9/18		Inspection of Unit by A.D.V.S. III Corps.	24
do	18/9/18		Evacuation of 23 animals to No 3 V.E.S. CARNOY. 1 N.C.O. & 3 men.	24
do	19/9/18		Evacuation of 30 animals to No 3 V.E.S. CARNOY. 1 N.C.O. & 5 men in charge.	24
do	20/9/18		Evacuation of 11 animals to No 3 V.E.S. CARNOY. 1 N.C.O. & 2 men in charge. Routine.	24
do	21/9/18		Routine	24
do	22/9/18		Station joins Div. B.E.I.	24
do	23/9/18		T.T.0715 Pte/Pfd. Robinson E.G. & TS.23859 Pte/Pfd Shepherd	24
Temp. Ref. Div. BS 1	24/9/18		proceed to No 2 Vety Hospital for training as Sgts. A.V.C. to Field Units.	24
do	25/9/18		10 animals evacuated to No 3 V.E.S. ALLAINES.	24
do	26/9/18		T.T.0717 Sgt. Doust. 2 A.V.C. reported for duty A.F.	24
do	27/9/18		14 days leave to England. T.S.14143. Pte. Shepherd T.S. A.V.C. proceeds on 14 days leave to England. 26/9 to 10/10/18.	24

A Campbell Capt
O.C. 2/1 Lond. M.V.S. 58 Div.

2/3/(LOND) M.V.S. 5th Divisional

WAR DIARY

or

INTELLIGENCE SUMMARY

(Erase heading not required.)

Army Form C. 2118.

Place	Date	Hour	Summary of Events and Information	Remarks and references to Appendices
Front Line Sec Bd 12.15	23/9/18		Section moves to new area at MONTAUBAN.	
"	24/9/18		Section moves to new area, returning at EDGE HILL and billeted at AUBIGNY, marching by road.	
"	25/9/18		to MINGOVAL. Setting for horses and accommodation for men. Fortree	
MINGOVAL	28/9/18		Evacuation of 1 animal to XVIII V.E.S.	
"	29/9/18		Section moves to new area at BOWVIGNY	
"	30/9/18		First stabling for horses and accommodation for men. Monthly Returns typewritten	

A Campbell Capt
O.C. 2/3 Lond M.V.S. 58 Divn.

WAR DIARY of **N°(LONDON) M.V.S. 58 Division**

or

INTELLIGENCE SUMMARY

Army Form C. 2118.

(Erase heading not required.)

Place	Date	Hour	Summary of Events and Information	Remarks and references to Appendices
B.n. VIGNY	1-10-18		Routine.	
"	2.10.18		Routine.	
"	3.10.18		Evacuation of 18 animals to N° 1 V.E.S. BARLIN. N.C.O. Y in men in charge.	
"	4.10.18		Inspection of unit by Lt.Col Nicol. D.D.V.S. 4 Corps. VIII Corps. Sgt Sergeant Sn. D.V.C. returned off 14 days leave to England.	
"	5.10.18		Pte 9388 Pte Hogg.J. SPINK S. A.V.C. Proceeds on 14 days leave to England. Pte 9869 Pte. 8gt. to 21 ⅖.	
"	6.10.18		Routine. Inspection of unit by Lt.Col Nicol. A.V.C. A.D.V.S. VIII Corps.	
"	7.10.18		Routine	
"	8.10.18		Routine collection & treatment of cases.	
"	9.10.18		Evacuation of 18 animals to N° 1 V.E.S. BARLIN. 1 N.C.O. & 3 men in charge. Sgt. 213343 Pte Watts H A.V.C. Proceeds to Headqrters III Corps for duty.	

J. Campbell CAPT.
O.C. 2/1 Lond. M.V.S. 58 Divn.

71st (LONDON) M.V.S.   WAR DIARY 58 DIVISION
or
INTELLIGENCE SUMMARY

Place	Date	Hour	Summary of Events and Information	Remarks and references to Appendices
BOUVIGNY	10.10.18		Lt. O.S.P.H. CORBISHLEY. P.A.V.C. proceeds on 14 days leave to England. 11.10.18 to 25.10.18.	
"	11.10.18		Newly returns received to L.H.D.N.S. 58 Divn.	
"	12.10.18		Routine.	
"			Evacuation of 12 animals to No.1 V.E.S. BARLIN. N.C.O. & 2 men in charge.	
"	13.10.18		Lt. SHAPPARD O.C. our returned to England.	
"			14 days leave to England.	
"			Routine	
"	14.10.18		Routine. Collection & statement of cases.	
"	15.10.18		Section moving to new area at LES BREBIS. Road littles stalling.	
LES BREBIS	16.10.18		Evacuation of 27 animals to No.1 V.E.S. BARLIN. 1 N.C.O. & 4 men in charge.	
"	17.10.18		Section moves to new area at CITE ST PIERRE. Huts on hire. Dug-outs for men.	
"	18.10.18		Newly returns — rendered to D.A.L.V.S. 58 Divn. D. Campbell	O.C. 71 Lond. M.V.S. 58 Divn.

47/3 LONDON. M.V.S. • 58 DIVISION •

WAR DIARY
or
INTELLIGENCE SUMMARY
(Erase heading not required.)

Army Form C. 2118.

Instructions regarding War Diaries and Intelligence Summaries are contained in F. S. Regs., Part II. and the Staff Manual respectively. Title Pages will be prepared in manuscript.

[Stamp: MOBILE VETY. SECTION 31 OCT 1918 58th LOND. DIVISION]

Place	Date	Hour	Summary of Events and Information	Remarks and references to Appendices
CITE ST PIERRE.	19/10/18		Section moves to new area at Mob. Ref. O23.C. Shut. No. A.	
MONTIGNY			No MONTIGNY. Food, staffing & billets. Evacuation of 12 animals to No 1 V.E.S. BARLIN. 1 N.C.O & men i/c charge.	
"	20/10/18		Section moves to new area at MONCHEAUX. 2 animals collected en route. Food staffing & billets.	
MONCHEAUX. 21/10/18			Section moves to new area at BERSEE. good staffing billets.	
BERSEE.	22/10/18		Collection & treatment of cases.	
BERSEE.	23/10/18		Posture. A.T. 0862 S/Sgt. S. SPINKS. a.21.L. returns off 14 days leave to England.	
"	24/10/18		Weekly Returns rendered to D.A.D.V.S. 58 Div.	
"	25/10/18		Inspection of Anl. by Lt. Col. the DOUGAL. a.D.L. a.D.V.S. 1st Corps. S.S.0707 Pte KILLICK F.G. proceeds on 14 days leave to England.	

J Campbell CAPT.
O.C. 57/1 Lond. M.V.S. 58 DIVn.

2/1st (London) M.V.S. 58 Div.

WAR DIARY
or
INTELLIGENCE SUMMARY
(Erase heading not required.)

Instructions regarding War Diaries and Intelligence Summaries are contained in F.S. Regs. Part II. and the Staff Manual respectively. Title pages will be prepared in manuscript.

Army Form C. 2118.

MOBILE VETY. SECTION
Date 8 OCT 1918
58th LOND. DIVISION

Place	Date	Hour	Summary of Events and Information	Remarks and references to Appendices
BERSEE	26/10/18		Evacuation of 18 animals to No 1 V.E.S. at BERCLAU. 1 N.C.O. + 3 men in charge.	
"	27/10/18		1 N.C.O. + 2 B213 rendered to Headqrs "F" 58 Division. 2 Animals conveyed by lorry Ambulance to 1 V.E.S. BERCLAU. 2 animals collected from French Inhabitant No NOMAIN.	
"	28/10/18		Posture. 3 animals destroyed carcase distributed to French Inhabitants of BERSEE. Hides sent to No 1 V.E.S.	
"	29/10/18		Section moves to new bil. at NOMAIN. Good starting + billets.	
NOMAIN	30/10/18		Posture. collection. treatment of cases. T.T.06794 Cpl BURBISHLEY returns off 14 days leave to England.	
"	31/10/18		Weekly Returns rendered to D.A.D.V.S. 58 Div. Evacuation of 14 animals to No 1 V.E.S. at GONDECOURT. 1 N.C.O. + 4 men in charge. TR15253 Pte MITCHELL F. A.V.C. Proceeds on 14 days leave to ENGLAND. Col of Pit clang the BASE.	

Camp Taylor Capt.
O.C. 2/1 Lond. M.V.S. 58 Div.

2/1 (London) M.V.S. 58 Division. WAR DIARY or INTELLIGENCE SUMMARY.

Army Form C. 2118.

Instructions regarding War Diaries and Intelligence Summaries are contained in F. S. Regs., Part II. and the Staff Manual respectively. Title pages will be prepared in manuscript.

(Erase heading not required.)

Place	Date	Hour	Summary of Events and Information	Remarks and references to Appendices
NOMAIN.	1/11/18		Routine, collection & treatment of cases.	DC
"	2/11/18		Evacuation of 13 animals to No 1 V.E.S. CONDECOURT. 1 animal conveyed by Float: 1 N.C.O. & 4 men in charge.	DC
"	3/11/18		Routine.	DC
"	4/11/18		Evacuation of 3 animals to No 1 V.E.S. CONDECOURT. 1 animal conveyed by Float. 2 men in charge.	DC
"	5/11/18		Evacuation of 10 animals to No 1 V.E.S. CONDECOURT, 1 N.C.O. & 2 men in charge.	DC
"	6/11/18		Routine, collection & treatment of cases.	DC
"	7/11/18		Weekly Returns rendered to D.A. of V.S. 58 Divn. General Inspection of Unit by Major General J. W. Ramsay. C.M.G. D.S.O. G.O.C. 58 Division.	DC
"	8/11/18		Routine.	DC
"	9/11/18		Section moves to new area at RUMEGIES.	DC
RUMEGIES	10/11/18		Routine. 2 cases admitted.	DC

J Campbell CAPT.
O.C. 2/1 Lond. M.V.S. 58 Divn.

2/1 (Lond) M.V.S. 58 Division

WAR DIARY
or
INTELLIGENCE SUMMARY
Army Form C. 2118.

(Erase heading not required.)

Instructions regarding War Diaries and Intelligence Summaries are contained in F. S. Regs., Part II. and the Staff Manual respectively. Title pages will be prepared in manuscript.

Place	Date	Hour	Summary of Events and Information	Remarks and references to Appendices
ROMEGIES.	10/11/18		Return moves to new area at BLEHARIES. 43 Remounts collected from LILLE.	DC
"	12/11/18		Return moves to new area at BELOEIL. Remounts conveyed by rail.	DC
BELOEIL.	13/11/18		Remounts issued to units in the field.	DC
"	14/11/18		Weekly Returns rendered to H.Q. D.V.S. 58 Div. Inspection of unit by the A.D.V.S. 1st Corps.	DC
"	15/11/18		Gunner. T.7.087. John STEWART. T.A.V.C. admitted to No 73 Fd Ambulance.	DC
"	16/11/18		A.F. B213. rendered to "Hughis A." 58 Division.	DC
"	17/20/11/18		Routine.	DC
"	21/11/18		Weekly Returns rendered to H.Q. D.V.S. 58 Division. 2 animals conveyed to No1 V.E.S. LA POSTERIE. by Mobile Ambulance.	DC
"	27/11/18		2 animals conveyed to No1 V.E.S. LA POSTERIE. by Mobile Ambulance.	DC

J Campbell CAPT.
O.C. 2/1 Lond. M V S. 58 Divn.

WAR DIARY or INTELLIGENCE SUMMARY

Army Form C. 2118.

2/1 (LOND) M.V.S.

Place	Date	Hour	Summary of Events and Information	Remarks and references to Appendices
BELLOEIL	23/11/18		Evacuation of 18 Animals to No 1 V.E.S. LA POSTERIE. 2 N.C.O's & 5 men in charge. A.F. B213 rendered to D.A.D.V.S. 58 Division.	—
"	24/11/18		Routine.	—
"	25/11/18		SS/15253 Pte Mitchell D.A.V.C. despatched to No 2 Vety Hospital Base for transfer to Home Establishment.	—
"	26/11/18		Routine.	—
"	27/11/18		Routine.	—
"	28/11/18		Weekly Returns rendered to D.A.D.V.S. 58 Division. SE/22872 Pte Gregory J.E. A.V.C. joined for duty from 2 Vety Hospital.	—
"	29/11/18		Veterinary returns to hand now at (THE TANNERY PERUWELZ) Good stabling - billets for men.	—
PERUWELZ	30/11/18		No 361483. Pte Minton F. 5/10 London Regt. attached for instruction in Vety work. Cash account rendered to O/C Divnl Army Serv. Corps.	—

O.O. 2/1 Lond. M.V.S. 58 Divn
J. Campbell
CAPT.

Army Form C. 2118.

2/1 (LONDON) M.V.S. WAR DIARY 58th Division.

or

INTELLIGENCE SUMMARY.

(Erase heading not required.)

Place	Date	Hour	Summary of Events and Information	Remarks and references to Appendices
PERUWELZ	1/12/18		Routine.	
"	2.12.18		Evacuation of 15 animals to N°1 V.E.S. 4 A. PASTERIE. 1 N.C.O. & 3 men in charge.	AC
"	3.12.18		1 animal destroyed "Gas Henenies" VP. carcase sold to local butcher for 250 frs.	AC
"	4.12.18.		T3.16243. Pte. Thompson. H.S. i.e.s. rejoined from hospital.	AC
"	5.12.18.		Kirkby Returns rendered to O.A.D.V.S. 58 Division. 1 Laden horse destroyed carcase sold to local butcher for 300 frs. Evacuation of 13 animals to N°1 V.E.S. 4A PASTERIE. 1 N.C.O. & 3 men in charge.	AC
"	6.12.18.		Routine.	AC
"	7.12.18.		Evacuation of 13 animals to N°1 V.E.S. 4A PASTERIE 1 N.C.O. & 3 men in charge.	AC
"	8/12/18.		T3.19714 Sgt. Salmon. R.B. i.e.s. reported for duty. T.70189 He THOMPSON H. i.e.s. rejoined from hospital.	AC
"	9/12/18		Routine.	AC
"	10-11/12/18		Routine.	AC

ACampbell CAPT.
O.C. 2/1 Lond. M.V.S. 58 Divn.

WAR DIARY or INTELLIGENCE SUMMARY

(Erase heading not required.)

Army Form C. 2118.

71st (LOND) M.V.S. 58th (London) Division

Instructions regarding War Diaries and Intelligence Summaries are contained in F.S. Regs., Part II. and the Staff Manual respectively. Title pages will be prepared in manuscript.

Place	Date	Hour	Summary of Events and Information	Remarks and references to Appendices
PERUWELZ	11/12/18		Weekly Returns rendered to D.A.D.V.S. 58 Division	24
"	13/12/18		General Routine, collection & treatment of sick and injured cases.	24
"	14/12/18		A.F.Z.12. Sgt. Jones 2nd S. interned 2/L R.E. proceed to England	24
"	"		A.F. B213 rendered re Hotchkiss "H" of Division	24
"			Inspection of Unit by Lt. Col. Drougal A.D.V.S. III Corps	24
"	15/12/18		Routine.	24
"	16/12/18		Evacuation of 15 animals to 1 V.E.S. 4 POSTERIE.	24
"			1 N.C.O. & 2 men in charge.	24
"	17/12/18		Routine.	24
"	18/12/18		A.F.B.213 & B.209 & Z.2.	24
"			Lt. Lukey M.E.C. proceeded to England for demobilization	24
"	19/12/18		Weekly Returns rendered to D.A.D.V.S. 58 Division	24
"			Butchery Account rendered to D.A.D.V.S. III Corps.	24
"	20/12/18		Evacuation of 18 animals to 1 V.E.S. 12 M. & POSTERIE 2 N.C.O's & 2 men in charge	24

A. Campbell CAPT.
O.C. 71 Lond. M.V.S. 58 Divn.

WAR DIARY or INTELLIGENCE SUMMARY

Army Form C. 2118.

2/1 (London) Mob. Vety. Section — 58th Division

(Erase heading not required.)

Place	Date	Hour	Summary of Events and Information	Remarks and references to Appendices
PERUWELZ	22/12/18		B213 removed to H.Q. 58 Division.	
"			No. 505 Pte. CHATTERTON W.V. transferred to sick from No. 2 Vety Hosp.	
"	23/12/18		Routine.	
"	24/12/18		Evacuation of 13 animals to No. 1 V.E.S. LA POSTERIE. 1 N.C.O. & 1 man in charge.	
"	25/12/18		Evacuation of 19 animals to No. 1 V.E.S. LA POSTERIE. 1 N.C.O. & 3 men in charge.	
"			Inspection of unit by Col. RODD A.V.C. D.D.V.S. 2nd Army.	
"			1 A.D.V.S. 1st Corps.	
"			General Routine.	
"	27/12/18		Fitteley Returns rendered to D.A.D.V.S. 58 Div.	
"	28/12/18		Monthly Returns rendered to D.A.D.V.S. 58 Div.	
"	29/12/18		M.T. B213 returned to H.Q. 58 Division.	
"	30/12/18		Routine.	
"	31/12/18		Evacuation of 5 horses to No. 1 V.E.S. LA POSTERIE. 1 N.C.O. & 2 men in charge.	
"	31/12/18		Routine. Foot account rendered to Lt. Henry the Bne. N Cavmy.	

CAPT.
O.C. 2/1 Lond. M.V.S. 58 Divn.

WAR DIARY 58 Division
M (London) Mob. Vety. Section

INTELLIGENCE SUMMARY

(Erase heading not required.)

Army Form C.—2118.

Place	Date	Hour	Summary of Events and Information	Remarks and references to Appendices
PERUWELZ	1/1/19		Evacuation of 13 animals to No 1 V.E.S, LA POSTERIE, 1.N.C.O. 6 men in charge. Weekly Returns rendered to- D.A.D.V.S. 58 Divn.	
"	2/1/19		48 animals collected from No 1 V.E.S. LA POSTERIE & brought into the M.V.S. at PERUWEZ for sale up till 4th Jany.	
"	3/1/19		Capt. HUTTON R.A.V.C. joined from No 1 V.E.S. to conduct Horse Sale on the 4th.	
"	4/1/19		Sale by auction at PERUWELZ, 71 animals disposed of by auction to persons in Divisional Units.	
"	5/1/19		Lecture, Capt. Hutton R.A.V.C. returned to- No 1 V.E.S.	
"	6/1/19		Classification reports rendered to units	
"	7/1/19		Do. Do.	
"	8/1/19		Do. Do.	
"	9/1/19		Do. Do.	
"	10/1/19		Weekly Returns rendered to- D.A.D.V.S. 58 Divn. 22 Brood Mares collected from Divisional Units for despatch to- ENGLAND.	
"	11/1/19		22 Brood Mares despatched to- No 1 V.E.S. LA POSTERIE en route for ENGLAND.	

J. Campbell CAPT.
O.C. M/1 Lond M.V.S. 58 Divn.

No.(Lond.) Mob. Vety. Section

WAR DIARY 58 Division
or
INTELLIGENCE SUMMARY.
(Erase heading not required.)

Army Form C. 2118.

Instructions regarding War Diaries and Intelligence Summaries are contained in F. S. Regs., Part II. and the Staff Manual respectively. Title pages will be prepared in manuscript.

Place	Date	Hour	Summary of Events and Information	Remarks and references to Appendices
PERUWELZ	11/1/19		Routine. No. 505 Pte CHATTERTON, W. R.A.V.C. Proceeded on 14 days leave to ENGLAND. 12/1/19 to 26/1/19.	DC
"	12/1/19		T.T.0693 Cpl PETCH, E.B. R.A.V.C. Granted extension of leave 16-26/1/19 for demobilization, authy Offr R.A.V.C. Records Warwick.	DC
"	13/1/19		Classification of animals in Divisional Units.	DC
"	14/1/19		Tr. 478 Pte NELSON, S. R.A.V.C. Joined for duty from No. 2 Vety. Hosp.	DC
"	"		Classification of animals in Divisional Units.	DC
"	16/1/19		Weekly Returns rendered to D.A.D.V.S. 58 Division. 78 animals evacuated from No. 1 V.E.S. for sale by auction in PERUWELZ. 1 N.C.O. & 15 men in charge.	DC
"	17/1/19		Routine. CAPT. HUTTON, R.A.V.C. Joined from No. 1 M.V.S.— returned late on ret. 18th.	DC
"	18/1/19		Sale by auction at PERUWELZ. 97 animals disposed of to Belgian Farmers.	DC
"	19/1/19		CAPT. HUTTON R.A.V.C. returned to No. 1 M.V.S.	DC

J. Campbell CAPT.
O.C. 2/1 Lond. M.V.S. 58 Divn.

WAR DIARY or INTELLIGENCE SUMMARY

Army Form C. 2118.

(Erase heading not required.)

1/1(London) Mob. Vety. Section   58 Division

Instructions regarding War Diaries and Intelligence Summaries are contained in F. S. Regs., Part II. and the Staff Manual respectively. Title pages will be prepared in manuscript.

MOBILE V.ETY. SECTION
58th LOND. DIVISION

Place	Date	Hour	Summary of Events and Information	Remarks and references to Appendices
PERONNE	20/1/19		Routine, Animals in Divisional Units inspected.	
"	21/1/19		Routine. Do	
"	22/1/19		Routine.	
"	23/1/19		General Routine	
"	24/1/19		Weekly Returns rendered to D.A.D.V.S. 58th Division	
"	25/1/19		Animals in Divisional Units inspected.	
"	26/1/19		Do Do R.97 SB 213	
"			rendered to H.Q. 58 Division.	
"	27/1/19		Information received that 17.0695 Pte P.707 E.C. R.A.V.C. has been demobilized & to states self strong & seemingly.	
"	28/1/19		General Routine	
"	29/1/19 } 30/1/19 }		Weekly conference held at M.V.S. to investigation of any animals, also inspection of any animals for investigation of any cases of lameness.	
"	30/1/19		Weekly Returns rendered to D.A.D.V.S. 58th Division	
"	31/1/19		5 horses (Riding) class Y instructed from Station to M.V. Base & for three Unfit for Embarkation, Suffering for France. Unfit for General Unsoundness & Eye trouble. Fit Base	

CAPT.

2/1st Lond: Mob: Vety. Section   58 N. Division.

WAR DIARY
or
INTELLIGENCE SUMMARY
(Erase heading not required.)

Army Form C. 2118.

Place	Date	Hour	Summary of Events and Information	Remarks and references to Appendices
PERUWELZ	1/2/19		Routine. A.F.B. 213. rendered to H.Qrs. 58 Div.	
	2/2/19		Routine	
	3/2/19		"	
	4/2/19		4 animals destroyed. carcases sold to local butcher.	
	5/2/19		2 animals destroyed. carcases sold to local butcher	
	6/2/19		S.S. 13699. Pte Christy T. R.A.V.C. dispatched to England for demobilisation.	
	7/2/19		Weekly returns rendered to D.A.D.V.S.	
	8/2/19		Routine. 16 Broon mares collected into M.V.S. for dispatch to No 1. V.E.S.	
	9/2/19		16 Mares & 1 occupied "Y" M. dispatched to No 1 V.E.S. for demobilisation. NCO & 2 men in charge	
	10/2/19		Routine.	
	11/2/19		"	
	12/2/19		Evacuation of 11 animals to No, 1 V.E.S. 1 N.C.O. & 2 men in charge.	
	13/2/19		3 Animals dispatched to 511 Coy. A.S.C. for duty. 1 replace "Y" animals evacuated to Base for demobilisation.	
	14/2/19		S.6. 19626. Pte Crossland H. R.A.V.C. admitted to Hospital	
	15/2/19		Weekly returns rendered to D.A.D.V.S. 58 Div.	
	16/2/19		Routine.	
	17/2/19		A.F.B. 213. rendered to H.Qrs. 58 Div. Routine	
	18/2/19		Inspection of 100 animals from 2 6 Bdge. A.F.A. of M.V.S. by A.D.V.S. 1 horsfe. to select animal for sale on the 22nd Routine. Inspection of Units under Vety. administration from 2/1st Vety. Sec.	
	19/2/19		3 Animals destroyed & sold to local butcher	
			" " " " "	

J Campbell CAPT.
O.C. 2/1 Lond. M.V.S. 58 DIVN.

2/1 Lond: Mob: Vety. Section. 58th Division.

Army Form C. 2118.

WAR DIARY
or
INTELLIGENCE SUMMARY.
(Erase heading not required.)

Instructions regarding War Diaries and Intelligence Summaries are contained in F. S. Regs., Part II. and the Staff Manual respectively. Title pages will be prepared in manuscript.

Place	Date	Hour	Summary of Events and Information	Remarks and references to Appendices
PERUWELZ.	20/2/19 2/2/19		Weekly Returns rendered to D.A.D.V.S. H.Q 58th Div. 88 Animals brought into M.V.S. from 26 Bde A.T.A. & Divisional Units. For sale on the 22nd inst at Peruwelz.	AE AE
	22/2/19		Sale of 97 animals at Peruwelz. Capt. Campbell. R.A.V.C. O/c Sale. Sale realised 80,086 francs, money paid into 7th Cashier. 1st Corps.	AE
	23/2/19		Routine. Inspection of 100 animals at Peruwelz. for sale on Sat: March 1st.	AE
	24/2/19		Animals brought into M.V.S.	AE
	25/2/19		Routine. Branding of animals. Evacuation of 3 animals, "Mange" to No 1 V.E.S. 2 men in charge. 2 Animals sold to local butcher & destroyed.	AE
	26/2/19		Weekly Returns rendered to D.A.D.V.S. 58 Div.	AE
	27/2/19		Routine. 20 Animals brought in from Divisional Units for sale on March 1st.	AE
	28/2/19		All animals branded & listed ready for sale. Sale account rendered to O/c Ebonring Kee. Base.	AE

D. Campbell CAPT.
O.C. 2/1 Lond. M.V.S. 58 Divn.

www.ingramcontent.com/pod-product-compliance
Lightning Source LLC
Chambersburg PA
CBHW081443160426
43193CB00013B/2369